150 CARDS
For All Seasons™

Edited by Vicki Blizzard

Annie's Attic®

150 CARDS
For All Seasons

Card making is taking the country by storm, and it's easy to see why. We can custom-create a card for a special person using whatever theme and colors we want, putting in whatever sentiment fits best. We are no longer limited to the cards we find in stores.

I especially love to create holiday cards. When I have time, I make each one individually, thinking about the

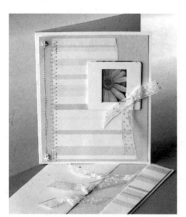

person or family that card is meant for. When time is short, I can create a group of similar cards in an evening—changing them slightly so that each person still gets a different card.

We've chosen 150 projects for this book to satisfy your craving for card designs. From simple to complex, you'll find cards for all sorts of occasions throughout the year. Make these projects as is or alter and personalize them to create just the card you need.

We enjoyed putting this book together for you, and we hope you like these projects as much as we do!

Warm regards,

Vicki Blizzard

CONTENTS

Staff
Editor: Vicki Blizzard
Associate Editor: Tanya Fox
Copy Supervisor: Michelle Beck
Copy Editors: Nicki Lehman, Mary O'Donnell
Technical Editor: Brooke Smith
Graphic Arts Supervisor: Ronda Bechinski
Graphic Artist: Edith Teegarden
Photography: Tammy Christian, Don Clark, Matthew Owen, Jackie Schaffel
Photo Stylists: Tammy Nussbaum, Tammy M. Smith

Annie's Attic
306 East Parr Road, Berne, IN 46711
©2006 Annie's Attic

TOLL-FREE ORDER LINE or to request a free catalog (800) 582-6643
Customer Service (800) 282-6643,
Fax (800) 882-6643
Pattern Services (260) 589-4000, ext. 333

Visit www.AnniesAttic.com

150 Cards for All Seasons is published by Annie's Attic, 306 East Parr Road, Berne, IN 46711, telephone (260) 589-4000. Printed in USA. Copyright © 2006 Annie's Attic. RETAIL STORES: If you would like to carry this pattern book or any other Annie's Attic publications, call the Wholesale Department at Annie's Attic to set up a direct account: (903) 636-4303. Toll-free order line or to request a free catalog (800) LV-ANNIE (800-582-6643). Customer Service: (800) AT-ANNIE (800-282-6643), Fax (800) 882-6643. Also, request a complete listing of publications available from Annie's Attic. Visit www.AnniesAttic.com.

Every effort has been made to ensure that the instructions in this pattern book are complete and accurate. We cannot, however, take responsibility for human error, typographical mistakes or variations in individual work.
Reprinting or duplicating the information, photographs or graphics in this publication by any means, including copy machine, computer scanning, digital photography email, personal Web site and fax, is illegal. Failure to abide by federal copyright laws may result in litigation and fines.

ISBN: 1-59635-070-9

Library of Congress Control Number:
2005935358

2 3 4 5 6 7 8 9

Labeled with Love

Design by MARY AYRES

Cut a 7½ x 9-inch rectangle from brown card stock; score and fold in half. Apply black ink along folded edge. Cut a 3 x 9-inch dark brown rectangle and apply black ink to left edge; glue along right side of card. Cut a 2⅞ x 9-inch rectangle from striped paper so that stripes run vertically; add black ink to left edge and adhere along right side of card.

Cut a 1½ x 3½-inch piece of gray textured card stock; apply black ink to edges and layer on top of a 1¾ x 3¾-inch light brown rectangle. Glue piece along bottom edge of card. Attach "L," "O," "V" and "E" alphabet stickers to black card stock; tear card stock around stickers. Add brown ink to sticker edges and glue piece on top of layered rectangles at bottom of card. Punch ¹⁄₁₆-inch holes at each end of word; attach brads.

For word tags, adhere six black label word stickers to tan parchment paper. Tear paper around words leaving space on left side for eyelets. Apply brown ink to edges; punch a ⅛-inch hole at left end of each tag and glue strips on an angle onto card. Punch another hole beside each tag; attach eyelets; insert burlap strands through eyelets and knot ends together.

To embellish envelope, cut a 1¼ x 3½-inch rectangle from striped paper; add brown ink to edges and layer on top of a 1½ x 3¾-inch dark brown rectangle. Add black ink to edges.

Adhere a black label word sticker to parchment paper; tear parchment paper around word and apply brown ink to edges. Punch a ¹⁄₁₆-inch hole at each end; glue word to layered rectangles and attach brads. Glue assembled piece to envelope and apply brown ink to edges. ∎

SOURCES: Striped paper and black label word stickers from K&Company; alphabet stickers from EK Success; Zip Dry paper adhesive from Beacon.

MATERIALS

Brown, dark brown, light brown, black and gray textured card stock
Tan parchment paper
Brown striped paper
Alphabet stickers
Black label word stickers
White envelope to fit a 3¾ x 9-inch card
Brown and black ink pads
6 burlap strands
4 round pewter mini brads
12 (⅛-inch) round antique gold eyelets and eyelet setter tool
Rotary tool and scoring blade
¹⁄₁₆- and ⅛-inch hole punches
Instant-dry paper adhesive

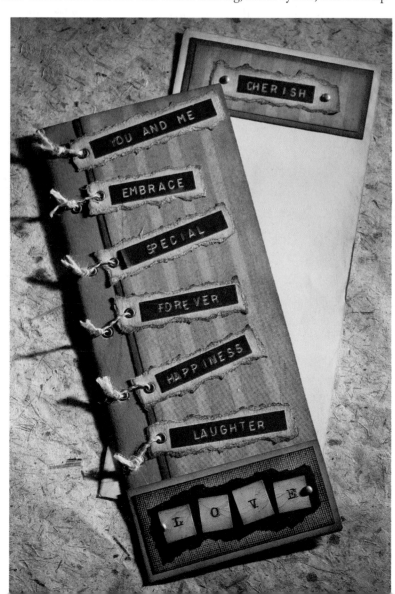

You Hold My Heart

Design by LINDA BEESON

MATERIALS

Olive green and brown
    card stock
Green/floral-print double-
    sided paper
Burgundy floral-print paper
Light green paper
Assorted letter stickers
Small tag sticker
Gold heart brad
Burgundy ribbon
Heart punch
Hole punch
Envelope template
Sandpaper
Glue stick

Score and fold a 5½ x 8½-inch piece of olive green card stock in half to form a 4¼ x 5½-inch card. Layer a 3¾ x 5-inch light green piece of paper onto a 4 x 5¼-inch piece of brown card stock. Cut three strips from burgundy floral-print paper in the following measurements: ½ x 3¾-inch, ³⁄₁₆ x 3¾-inch and 2¼ x 3¾-inch. Adhere the ½-inch-wide strip along the left edge of light green paper; adhere the ³⁄₁₆-inch-wide strip ⅛ inch from first strip. Tear one long edge of remaining strip and adhere ⅛ inch from second strip.

Punch two holes in lower right corner; thread a piece of ribbon through holes from front to back. Cross ribbon ends over each other and thread back through to front. Trim ends in V-notches. Attach heart brad on top of ribbon; glue assembled piece to card.

Referring to photo, use tag and letter stickers to spell "you hold my heart" on card.

Use envelope template to trace and cut an envelope from green/floral-print double-sided paper with green as the outside of the envelope. Sand all edges. Score and fold lines; glue bottom and side flaps.

Punch a heart on left side of envelope flap. Lightly trace heart onto another piece of double-sided paper; cut heart out making it slightly larger. Glue heart to backside of envelope flap allowing contrasting pattern to show through punched area. ∎

SOURCES: Coluzzle envelope template from Provo Craft; double-sided paper and burgundy floral-print paper from Daisy D's Paper Co.; heart punch from Emagination Crafts; stickers from EK Success, Wordsworth and Creative Imaginations.

Adore

Design by GAYLE HODGINS

Cut an 8½ x 8¾-inch piece of brown/gold patterned paper; score and fold in half to form a 4⅜ x 8½-inch card. Cut a 3⅛ x 5⅜-inch piece of a different patterned paper than card. Ink edges of paper and card with black ink. Glue smaller piece in upper left corner; glue crate label on the right side of card.

Use fingers to apply sheer gold glaze to metal heart plaque and photo corners; set aside to dry. Use letter stickers to spell "LOVE" in upper left corner and "you" vertically alongside left edge of crate label. Stamp "Adore" across bottom of card with pearlescent gold ink. Use craft glue to adhere metal heart plaque in upper left corner; glue metal photo corners on upper and lower right corners of crate label.

SOURCES: Patterned papers and alphabet stickers from Basic Grey; rubber stamps from MoBe' Stamps; Brilliance ink pad from Tsukineko Inc.; vintage fruit crate label from Ephemera Vintage Graphics; metal heart plaque and photo corners from Making Memories; Paper Plus Sheer Gold Glaze from Delta.

MATERIALS
- Brown/gold coordinating patterned papers
- Vintage fruit crate label
- Small metal heart plaque
- 2 gold metal photo corners
- Letter stickers
- Alphabet rubber stamps
- Pearlescent gold and black ink pads
- Sheer gold glaze
- Glue stick
- Craft glue

MATERIALS

Pink striped paper

Black textured and pink
    card stock

Pink twine

Tiara die cut

Spiral heart rubber stamp

Black ink pad

"I Love You" printed ribbon

Pink polka-dot ribbon

Silver moulding corners

Small washer eyelet

8 clear round rhinestones

Clear marquis rhinestone

White opaque fine-tip
    marker (optional)

Stapler with dark pink
    staples

Envelope template

Paper trimmer

Gem adhesive

Adhesive dots

Double-sided tape

Glue stick

Computer font (optional)

Fairytale Dreams

Design by KATHLEEN PANEITZ

Cut black textured card stock 4¼ x 10 inches; score and fold in half. Adhere a 2½ x 4¼-inch piece of pink striped paper toward bottom of card; trim edges. Adhere a piece of polka-dot ribbon across top of striped paper; wrap ribbon ends inside card and secure with adhesive dots. Staple "I Love You" ribbon vertically along right edge of card with dark pink staples. Adhere tiara across top of card; adhere rhinestones to tiara with gem adhesive. Attach moulding corners to top two corners.

Use a computer or hand-print "Once in a while, right in the middle of an ordinary life, love gives us a fairytale" or desired fairytale message onto black card stock using white ink. Cut a tag shape around message and adhere a small strip of striped paper across top of tag; attach washer eyelet and tie pink twine through eyelet. Adhere tag across bottom portion of card.

For envelope, use template to cut an envelope from pink card stock. Fold and assemble envelope with double-sided tape. Stamp swirled heart image onto pink striped paper; cut a rectangle around image and apply black ink to edges. Adhere rectangle in lower left corner of envelope. ∎

SOURCES: Patterned paper from Rusty Pickle; printed ribbon, moulding corners and colored staples from Making Memories; tiara die cut from Deluxe Designs; washer eyelet from Creative Impressions; rhinestones from The Beadery; envelope template from Lasting Impressions for Paper Inc.; rubber stamp from Hero Arts.

Locket of Love

Design by SANDRA GRAHAM SMITH

Cut navy card stock 5½ x 8½ inches; score and fold in half. Stamp love sentiment randomly over card with watermark ink. Referring to photo, use stamp positioner to determine correct placement of hearts. Stamp three hearts along right card edge; emboss top and bottom hearts with copper embossing powder. Emboss middle heart with silver embossing powder. Trim edge following heart outlines.

Stamp heart lock onto navy card stock and emboss with copper embossing powder; cut out lock. Cut out small keyhole with craft knife. Stamp keys onto navy card stock; emboss with silver embossing powder. Cut out with craft knife. Punch two small holes at bottom of heart lock; punch a hole at top of each key. Thread a jump ring onto each key; attach to lock. Use adhesive foam square to attach lock to card; secure keys with glue stick.

Use a computer or hand-print "Key to my heart" onto white card stock; trim a rectangle around words and layer onto copper card stock. Trim leaving a small border; glue to card above lock.

To embellish envelope, stamp swirled heart twice onto left side; emboss top heart copper and bottom heart silver. Stamp a key image onto envelope flap; emboss silver. ∎

SOURCES: VersaMark ink pad from Tsukineko Inc.; swirled heart stamp from Delta/Rubber Stampede; keys and heart lock stamps from Stampin' Up!.

MATERIALS

White, navy and copper
  card stock
4⅜ x 5¾-inch navy
  envelope
Watermark ink pad
Rubber stamps: swirled
  heart, heart lock,
  2 keys and love
  sentiment
Copper and silver
  embossing powder
2 silver jump rings
Stamp positioner
Small hole punch
Craft knife
Embossing heat tool
Adhesive foam squares
Glue stick
Computer font (optional)

Heart Strings

DIAGRAM ON PAGE 149

Design by SHARON REINHART

MATERIALS

- 12 x 12-inch sage green card stock
- Pale pink card stock
- Rose patterned paper
- Adhesive laminate sheet
- Ivory envelope to fit a 4¼ x 5½-inch card
- ³⁄₁₆-inch-wide ivory satin ribbon
- Pink blending filament thread
- "Love" and foliage rubber stamps
- Green iridescent embossing powder
- Sage green ink pad
- Small heart punch
- Scallop-edge heart punch
- Ribbon slot punch
- Decorative-edge scissors
- Paper trimmer
- Bone folder
- Embossing heat tool
- Cellophane tape
- Glue stick

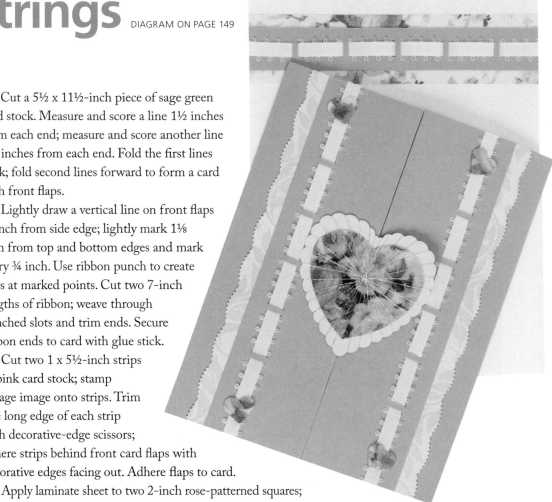

Cut a 5½ x 11½-inch piece of sage green card stock. Measure and score a line 1½ inches from each end; measure and score another line 3⅝ inches from each end. Fold the first lines back; fold second lines forward to form a card with front flaps.

Lightly draw a vertical line on front flaps ¼ inch from side edge; lightly mark 1⅛ inch from top and bottom edges and mark every ¾ inch. Use ribbon punch to create slots at marked points. Cut two 7-inch lengths of ribbon; weave through punched slots and trim ends. Secure ribbon ends to card with glue stick.

Cut two 1 x 5½-inch strips of pink card stock; stamp foliage image onto strips. Trim one long edge of each strip with decorative-edge scissors; adhere strips behind front card flaps with decorative edges facing out. Adhere flaps to card.

Apply laminate sheet to two 2-inch rose-patterned squares; use pattern provided to trace heart on backside of squares and cut out. Punch four small hearts from leftover laminate rose paper. Adhere small hearts to card at top and bottom of woven ribbon.

Punch a scallop-edge heart from pink card stock; center and adhere a laminate heart to pink heart. Working from spool, attach pink blending filament thread end to backside of punched heart with cellophane tape; working clockwise, begin to wrap heart with thread until heart is completed. Secure thread at back with tape. Adhere wrapped heart to left flap on card; adhere remaining laminate heart to the backside of heart inside card.

Center and adhere a 3¾ x 5-inch piece of rose patterned paper inside card; punch a scallop-edge heart from pink card stock. Stamp and emboss "Love" onto heart.

To embellish envelope, cut a 1-inch-wide strip of rose patterned paper; adhere to left side of envelope and trim edges even. Cut a ⅝-inch-wide strip of sage green card stock; punch ribbon slots every ¾ inch and weave a 5½-inch piece of ribbon through slots. Trim ribbon and card stock ends to fit along left edge of envelope. Adhere strip onto rose-patterned strip. ∎

SOURCES: Patterned paper from The C-Thru Ruler Co./Deja Views; self-adhesive vinyl laminate sheet from Brodart; Love cube rubber stamp from Serendipity Stamps; pearl embossing powder from Ranger; scallop-edge heart punch from Uchida of America; ribbon punch from McGill Inc.

Etched in Stone

Design by SHARON REINHART

Score and fold a 5½ x 8½-inch piece of opalescent cream card stock in half to form a 4¼ x 5½-inch card. Stamp Italian poetry image diagonally onto right side of card; emboss with rust embossing powder. Set aside.

Stamp and emboss two columns and one decorative heart onto opalescent cream card stock; cut out images. Adhere one column on the left side of card lining up bottom edges; adhere remaining column as a mirror image to first one lining up column's bottom edge with the top edge of card. Adhere heart on top of columns with adhesive foam tape.

Punch two hearts from opalescent cream card stock; punch three hearts from opalescent brown card stock. Adhere cream hearts to the center of decorative heart with foam tape. Adhere brown hearts randomly over poetry.

For envelope, place an adhesive paper note in center to mask off address area. Stamp poetry image twice diagonally onto envelope; emboss. Remove adhesive note. Stamp and emboss decorative heart onto opalescent cream card stock; cut out heart and adhere in lower left corner. ∎

SOURCES: Decorative heart rubber stamp from Magenta Rubber Stamps; Italian poetry stamp from Hero Arts; column stamp from Laughing Moon Rubber Stamps; adhesive foam tape from 3M.

MATERIALS

Opalescent cream and opalescent brown card stock

Cream envelope to fit a 4¼ x 5½-inch card

Rubber stamps: decorative heart, Italian poetry and decorative column

Clear embossing ink

Rust embossing powder

Small heart punch

Small adhesive paper note

Embossing heat tool

Adhesive foam tape

Glue stick

Celebrate Card Folder

Design by LINDA BEESON

MATERIALS

- Red floral-print paper
- Black/ivory floral-print paper
- Definition print paper
- Red card stock
- Notecard holder die with die-cut machine
- Brown envelopes to fit 4¼ x 5½-inch cards
- Slide mounts
- Black letter stickers
- Red silk flower
- Decorative black metal flower
- Black mini brad
- Black ink pad
- "Celebrate" rub-on transfer
- Black/ivory gingham ribbon
- Glue stick

Die-cut notecard holder once from red floral-print paper and once from black/ivory floral-print paper; layer papers wrong sides together. Cut an 18-inch piece of ribbon and place it between the papers letting approximately 7 inches extend out on each side; glue papers together. Score and fold lines; fold up pockets and glue to secure.

Cover a slide mount with black/ivory paper; cut out opening. Wrap and adhere excess paper around edges. Transfer "celebrate" along left edge of slide mount. Apply black ink to edges of silk flower; place decorative metal flower in center of silk flower and attach to slide mount with black mini brad. Cut a piece of definition print paper; adhere to backside of slide mount. Glue slide mount to front of notecard holder.

To make notecards, cut a 5½ x 8½-inch piece of red card stock. Score and fold in half. Glue a 4 x 5¼-inch piece of red floral-print paper to card. Cover slide mount with black/ivory floral-print paper in same manner as for front of holder. Wrap a piece of ribbon around left side of slide mount; tie a knot and trim ends. Adhere a piece of definition print paper to reverse side of slide mount; attach desired initial sticker. Center and glue to card. Repeat for desired amount of notecards; place notecards and envelopes in holder. ∎

SOURCES: Floral-print paper from Anna Griffin Inc.; definition print paper from Li'l Davis Designs; die-cut machine and die from AccuCut; slide mounts from DMD Inc.; Lost Art Treasures metal flower from American Tag; rub-on transfer from Making Memories; letter stickers from Doodlebug Design Inc.

Love Swirl

Design by SUSAN HUBER

Cut a 5½ x 8½-inch piece of yellow card stock; score and fold in half. Cut a 3¾ x 5-inch piece of white embossed card stock. Cut yellow polka-dot paper to 3 x 4 inches; center and tape brass stencil to yellow polka-dot paper. Apply stencil paste with palette knife; carefully remove stencil and immediately sprinkle with glitter. Let dry. Attach polka-dot piece to white embossed rectangle by punching a ⅛-inch hole through each corner and setting eyelets.

String "L," "O," "V" and "E" alphabet beads onto twine; tie a small knot between each bead. Insert twine ends into bottom eyelets; tie each end into a knot to secure. Attach piece to card.

Use envelope template to cut an envelope from white embossed card stock; score and fold lines. Assemble with glue stick. ∎

SOURCES: Card stock, paper and brass stencil from Lasting Impressions for Paper Inc.; alphabet beads from Westrim Crafts; stencil embossing paste from Dreamweaver Stencils; scallop-edge envelope template from Printworks.

MATERIALS

Yellow card stock
White embossed polka-dot card stock
Yellow polka-dot paper
4 (⅛-inch) white eyelets
Twine
Ultra-fine glitter
Alphabet beads
Scallop-edge envelope template to fit a 4¼ x 5½-inch card
Brass heart stencil
⅛-inch hole punch
Opaque stencil embossing paste
Palette knife
Removable tape
Glue stick

Kiss Me Goodnight

Design by S A N D R A   G R A H A M   S M I T H

MATERIALS

5½ x 8½-inch purple
  card stock
Small piece of white
  card stock
4⅜ x 5¾-inch purple
  envelope
Love-themed vellum
  sentiments
Mini vellum envelope
⅛-inch pewter eyelets
  with eyelet setter tool
3 cancelled "Love"
  postage stamps
Lips rubber stamp
Ink pads: watermark
  and deep purple
Small hole punch
Double-sided tape

Score and fold purple card stock in half to form a 4¼ x 5½-inch card. Randomly stamp lips image onto card with watermark ink. Cut out desired vellum sentiments; attach mini vellum envelope in upper left corner with double-sided tape. Referring to photo, attach vellum sentiments with eyelets. Stamp lips image onto white card stock with purple ink; cut out and attach to vellum envelope. Adhere postage stamps to card.

To embellish envelope, stamp lips image onto front of envelope and one on envelope flap with watermark ink; attach a postage stamp and vellum sentiment in lower left corner. ■

SOURCES: PeelnStick double-sided tape from Therm O Web; rubber stamp from Delta/Rubber Stampede; VersaMark ink pad from Tsukineko Inc.; Fresh Verse vellum sentiments from The C-Thru Ruler Co.

Carrot Express
DIAGRAMS ON PAGE 149

Design by LORETTA MATEIK

Cut a 5½ x 8½-inch piece of green card stock; score and fold in half. Use a computer or hand-print "...Easter" in upper left corner and "Wishes..." in upper right corner on top of card. Adhere a 2½ x 5-inch pale green rectangle toward bottom of card.

Use pattern provided to trace bunny head onto white embossed card stock; outline with black marker and cut out along marker edge. Add bunny eye with black marker.

Use a computer or hand-print "...Carrot Express..." onto orange card stock; use pattern provided to trace a carrot around message. Cut out carrot; add detail lines with black marker and run through paper crimper.

Cut small strips halfway into paper ribbon; fold and attach to back of carrot. Adhere bunny head to carrot referring to photo for placement; attach assembled carrot car to card. Adhere buttons to carrot. Roll pompom in pink chalk; adhere to bunny for nose.

For envelope, use markers and carrot pattern to draw a slightly smaller version of carrot car along bottom edge. ■

SOURCES: Embossed card stock from Lasting Impressions for Paper Inc.

MATERIALS

Green, pale green and
    orange card stock
White embossed polka-
    dot card stock
Pink chalk
3mm white pompom
2 (1-inch-diameter)
    round buttons
Small piece green
    paper ribbon
Black, orange and
    green markers
Paper crimper
Paper adhesive
Computer font (optional)

Easter Greetings

Design by LORETTA MATEIK

DIAGRAMS ON PAGE 149

MATERIALS

Pale green, green, dark green, pink and white card stock

White embossed polka-dot card stock

Daisy punch

Decorative corner punch

2 (3mm) white pompoms

Pink chalk

Black, pink and green markers

Adhesive dots

Glue stick

Computer font (optional)

Score and fold a 5½ x 8½-inch piece of dark green card stock in half to form a 4¼ x 5½-inch card. Cut a 4 x 5¼-inch rectangle of pale green card stock; punch decorative corners in rectangle and adhere to card.

Using provided patterns, trace and cut bunny sections from white embossed card stock; outline edges and draw facial details with black marker. Color one white pompom with pink chalk; adhere to bunny face as nose. Use foam dots to adhere bunny together. Adhere bunny to lower right corner of card.

Punch a daisy from pink card stock; fold in half. Using provided patterns, trace and cut a stem and leaves from green card stock. Referring to photo, adhere stem, leaves and daisy to lower left corner of card. Use a computer or hand-print "Easter Greetings" onto pale green card stock; cut a rectangle around words and layer onto pink and green card stock, trimming a border on each. Adhere to top of card.

If desired, use markers to draw a small flower with leaves on front of envelope. ∎

SOURCES: Embossed card stock from Lasting Impressions for Paper Inc.; daisy punch from Stampin' Up!; decorative corner punch from Uchida of America.

Daisy Line-Up

Design by S A N D R A   G R A H A M   S M I T H

Cut a 5½ x 8½-inch piece of yellow card stock; score and fold in half. Cut two ½-inch-wide strips from pink card stock and one ½-inch-wide strip from mint green card stock. Referring to photo, glue strips to card.

Punch two pink daisies, five mint green daisies and two yellow daisies. Glue yellow daisies to mint green card stock; glue one mint green daisy to pink card stock. Trim approximately 1-inch squares around daisies. Punch a ⅛-inch hole through the center of each daisy; set a yellow eyelet in each pink and green daisy and a pink eyelet in each yellow daisy.

Use a computer or hand print "Celebrate Spring!" on white paper; cut a rectangle around each word. Glue "Celebrate" onto pink card stock; glue "Spring!" onto mint green card stock. Trim a 1-inch square around each word. Referring to photo, glue word and flower squares to card. Secure remaining daisies to card with craft glue.

To embellish envelope, cut ½-inch-wide strips of pink and yellow card stock; glue a yellow strip across bottom front of envelope and a pink strip down left side. Trim edges even. Punch a daisy from mint green and yellow card stock; glue daisies to 1-inch squares in opposite colors. Glue squares to pink strip.

Glue a pink strip across envelope flap; trim edges. Punch a daisy from yellow card stock; glue to a 1-inch mint green square. ■

MATERIALS

Card stock: yellow, pink
    and mint green
White printer paper
White envelope to fit a
    5½ x 4¼-inch card
7 yellow and 2 pink
    (⅛-inch) round eyelets
    with eyelet setter tool
Small daisy punch
⅛-inch hole punch
Glue stick
Craft glue
Computer font (optional)

Stripes & Petals

Design by TAMI MAYBERRY

MATERIALS

Pink/orange striped
   double-sided and
   orange card stock
Die-cutting tool with large
   and medium daisy dies
³⁄₁₆-inch-wide bright pink
   ribbon
Dark pink ink pad
Small alphabet stamps
2 self-adhesive threaded
   orange buttons
Envelope template to fit
   an 8 x 5-inch card
Sandpaper
Glue stick

Cut an 8 x 12-inch piece of double-sided card stock; score a horizontal line 2 inches from top and another horizontal line 5 inches from bottom. Fold on scored lines with top flap overlapping bottom flap. Adhere ribbon along bottom edge of top flap; trim ends. Lightly sand card edges.

Die-cut one large and two medium daisies from double-sided card stock; set aside one medium daisy for use on envelope. Lightly sand edges of the two remaining daisies on pink side. Layer daisies and attach button in center. Glue layered daisies on left side of card, overlapping top flap. ***Note:*** *Be careful not to adhere top flap when adhering daisies.*

Stamp desired sentiment onto orange card stock; cut a rectangle around words. Tear off top and bottom edges. Adhere in lower right corner.

For envelope, use template to trace and cut an envelope from double-sided card stock, with striped side face up. Score and fold envelope flaps; glue side and bottom flaps together.

Attach self-adhesive button to remaining daisy on pink side. Cut a 5⅞ x 3¾-inch rectangle from orange card stock; tear off top edge. Glue to envelope; glue daisy to left side of orange rectangle. ■

SOURCES: Double-sided card stock from Making Memories; dies and die-cutting tool from Sizzix/Ellison; alphabet stamps and buttons from EK Success; Coluzzle envelope template from Provo Craft.

It's Spring DIAGRAM ON PAGE 149

Design by KATHLEEN PANEITZ

Cut a 12 x 7½-inch piece of yellow textured card stock. With long side laying parallel on work surface, score a vertical line 2 inches from right end; score another vertical line 4 inches from right end. Score a vertical line 2 inches from left end; score a vertical line 4 inches from left end. Fold the lines 4 inches from ends inward; fold remaining scored lines outward.

Cut a piece of daffodil print paper ¼ inch smaller on all sides than yellow textured card stock. Lay daffodil print paper on scored card stock; score and fold daffodil print paper on same lines.

Referring to diagram, attach a ¹⁄₁₆-inch gold eyelet on inside fold 1⅜ inches from top edge on daffodil print paper.

Attach daffodil sticker to transparency; trim a rectangle around sticker leaving room for eyelets. Attach ¹⁄₁₆-inch gold eyelets to top corners of transparency. Thread yellow floss through eyelets; thread loose ends of floss through eyelets on daffodil print paper and secure with knots on reverse side. ***Note:** When threading floss through eyelets, close daffodil print paper to determine desired length of floss. Length of floss will determine how low daffodil sticker will hang.*

Line up assembled daffodil print paper to scored yellow card stock; adhere outside edges. Set washer eyelets on outside edges of card; wrap yellow ribbon around card and thread through washer eyelets. Tie a bow to shut card; trim ends. Transfer "It's Spring" onto front flaps.

Use envelope template to trace and cut an envelope from glittered daffodil print paper; score and fold lines. ***Note:** Template measurements may need to be adjusted slightly to fit card.* Glue side and bottom flaps together. ∎

SOURCES: Daffodil print paper and sticker from K&Company; eyelets from Creative Impressions; rub-on transfers from Li'l Davis Designs; envelope template from The C-Thru Ruler Co.

MATERIALS

Daffodil print paper
Daffodil print
    glittered paper
Yellow textured card stock
Transparency sheet
Dimensional glittered
    daffodil sticker
Envelope template to fit
    a 4 x 7½-inch card
¹⁄₁₆-inch gold eyelets
Silver washer eyelets
Yellow floss
Small rectangle alphabet
    rub-on transfers
1-inch-wide sheer
    yellow ribbon
Eyelet setter tool
Stylus
Glue stick

Appreciation

Design by KATHLEEN PANEITZ

MATERIALS

White card stock

Brightly colored floral
    patterned paper

"Appreciation" definition

Light pink ink pad

Pink mini brads

"thanks" rub-on transfer

Orange acrylic
    embellishment

1½-inch-wide pink/orange
    plaid ribbon

Label maker with orange
    label tape

Envelope template to fit a
    6¼ x 4⅛-inch envelope

Glue stick

Double-sided tape

Cut a 6¼ x 8¼-inch piece of white card stock; score and fold in half. Cut a 6¼ x 4⅛-inch piece of patterned paper.

Trim a rectangle around "Appreciation" definition; rub light pink ink on edges of rectangle. Referring to photo for placement, glue to patterned piece of paper.

Transfer "thanks" onto orange acrylic embellishment. Attach embellishment above definition panel with double-sided tape; insert mini brads in each end of embellishment.

Use label maker to make a "for all you do" orange label; attach below definition. Glue assembled piece of paper to card. Cut a piece of ribbon; tie into a knot and trim ends into V-notches. Attach in upper left corner of card with double-sided tape.

Use envelope template to trace and cut an envelope from patterned paper; score and fold dashed lines. Glue side and bottom flaps together. ∎

SOURCES: Patterned paper from Scrappy Cat; rub-on transfer from Making Memories; acrylic embellishment from Junkitz; envelope template from The C-Thru Ruler Co.

Happy Day

Design by LINDA BEESON

Score and fold a 5½ x 11-inch piece of dark coral card stock in half to form a 5½-inch square card. Glue a 5¼ x 3½-inch piece of striped paper toward bottom of card.

Cut a 4¼-inch square from pink floral paper. Attach "happy day" sticker to white card stock; trim a triangle around sticker and layer onto orange card stock. Trim edges, leaving a small border. Glue onto floral square.

Punch a flower from dark coral card stock; punch a ⅛-inch hole in flower center. Wrap ribbon around floral square; thread both ribbon ends through flower and tie a knot. Trim ends. Transfer "SPRING" onto left side of ribbon.

Glue assembled piece to orange card stock; trim edges, leaving a small border. Glue to card.

Use envelope template to trace and cut an envelope from striped paper; score and fold lines. Glue side and bottom flaps together.

Punch a flower from dark coral card stock; punch a ¾-inch circle from coral card stock. Punch a ⅛-inch hole through flower center and top of circle. Stamp desired initial on circle; thread ribbon through circle and flower. Tie a knot and trim ends. ∎

SOURCES: Patterned papers and rub-on transfer from Chatterbox; sticker from Wordsworth; envelope template from Papers by Catherine.

MATERIALS

Card stock: orange, white, coral and dark coral
Pink striped and pink floral patterned papers
Clear "happy day" sticker
"Spring" rub-on transfer
Alphabet stamps
Black ink pad
½-inch-wide coral ribbon
Large flower punch
¾-inch circle punch
⅛-inch hole punch
Envelope template to fit a 5½-inch square card
Glue stick

Triangle Explosion

DIAGRAM ON PAGE 151

Design by BARBARA PELAK

MATERIALS

White and coral card stock
Coral ink pad
Rubber stamps: rose,
   speckle dots and
   "Have A Great Day!"
⅞-inch-wide sheer white
   ribbon
⅛-inch hole punch
Craft knife
Glue stick

Using pattern provided, cut out rounded square from white card stock; randomly stamp rose image onto square. Fill in areas with speckle dot image.

Score and fold square in half with patterned sides facing each other. Open square up and fold in half diagonally with white sides facing each other. Open one more time and fold in half diagonally, white sides facing each other.

Using pattern provided, trace and cut closure flap from coral card stock. Punch two ⅛-inch holes as indicated. Cut a 6-inch length of ribbon; thread ribbon through punched holes, beginning from the front. Wrap ribbon ends across each other and thread ends back through opposite holes. Trim ends diagonally.

Score and fold dashed line on closure flap; glue scored area at top of rounded square on stamped side. Use a craft knife to cut out small triangle as indicated on rounded square pattern.

Stamp "Have A Great Day!" inside card. Push sides inward and card will fold up following folds. Insert closure flap into triangle. ■

SOURCES: Rubber stamps from Stampin' Up!.

A Special Thank You

Design by STACEY STAMITOLES

Cut an 8½ x 5½-inch piece of green card stock; score and fold in half. Cut an 8 x 5-inch piece of ivory card stock; score and fold in half. Place the green card inside the ivory card; apply double-sided tape along folded edge only to adhere layers. Punch three pairs of holes along folded edge at top, center and bottom.

Stamp flower image onto pale yellow card stock with pink and green inks; watercolor flower by using watercolor pencils and blender pen. Let dry. Trim a 2⅛ x 3⅞-inch rectangle around flower; rub green ink on edges. Transfer "Thank You" at bottom of rectangle. Layer rectangle onto a 3¾ x 4⅝-inch floral patterned rectangle. Glue layered rectangle onto card.

Cut a small strip of floral patterned paper approximately 3½ x 2 inches; roll strip up lengthwise. Remove bottom cap from pen and insert rolled paper inside pen barrel around ink cartridge. Replace bottom cap.

Thread green ribbon through center set of holes in card; tie into a knot and trim ends. Thread ivory ribbon through the top and bottom sets of holes; position pen beside card and wrap ivory ribbons around pen. Tie knots and trim ends.

To embellish envelope, use envelope flap as a template to trace onto floral patterned paper. Cut out envelope flap from floral patterned paper and glue inside flap on premade envelope.

Cut a 5¾ x 1-inch strip of floral patterned paper; adhere along bottom edge on front of envelope. If not mailing envelope through postal system, cut a 1¼ x 1⅛-inch rectangle from floral patterned paper and adhere in upper right corner on front of envelope. ■

SOURCES: Patterned paper from Design Originals; rubber stamp from Hampton Art; rub-on transfer from What's New International/Scrap-Ease.

MATERIALS

Card stock: green, pale yellow and ivory
Floral patterned paper
Daisy with stem rubber stamp
Green and pink ink pads
Watercolor pencils
Blender pen
"Thank You" rub-on transfer
Ivory envelope to fit a 4¼ x 5½-inch card plus an attached pen
⅜-inch-wide ivory ribbon
⅜-inch-wide green striped ribbon
Ink pen with clear barrel
⅛-inch circle punch
Double-sided tape
Glue stick

Hi, Friend!

Design by JULIE EBERSOLE

MATERIALS

Card stock: light purple,
   purple
Purple vellum
5¾ x 4⅜-inch
   white envelope
Rubber stamps: flower stem,
   small decorative-edge
   frame, "hi, friend."
Ink pads: dark purple
   chalk, green chalk,
   black pigment
Metal-edge vellum
   round tag
Ribbon: ³⁄₁₆-inch-wide
   green with white
   stitching
Yellow eyelet with eyelet
   setting tool
Punches: ⅛-inch circle,
   small pompom,
   medium pompom
Craft knife
Glue stick

Cut a 4¼ x 8½-inch piece of light purple card stock; score and fold in half. Using dark purple ink, stamp decorative-edge frame in upper left corner of card front. Use craft knife to cut a 1¹⁄₁₆ x 1⅜-inch window from center of frame image.

Use green ink to stamp flower stem inside card, positioning it to show through frame window. Punch a small pompom from purple card stock; place pompom at top of flower stem. Punch a ⅛-inch hole through pompom and card. Set eyelet.

Use black ink to stamp "hi, friend." on metal-edge tag. Thread ribbon through tag; wrap ribbon around card front, positioning metal-edge tag on right side. Knot ends together on right side; trim ends.

For envelope, punch a medium pompom through right side of envelope. Cut a 1⅜ x 4¼-inch strip of purple vellum; apply adhesive along top and bottom edges on both sides of vellum. Adhere vellum inside envelope, covering punched pompom openings. Square card will fit in opening left inside envelope. ■

SOURCES: Rubber stamps from A Muse Artstamps; pompom punches from EK Success.

Butterfly Wishes

Design by KAREN ROBINSON

MATERIALS
Card stock: dark green,
   pale green and beige
Green leaf-print paper
Green patterned paper
Green butterfly stickers
"Get Well Soon" stamp
4 gold round brads
Envelope template to fit a
   4½ x 6¼-inch card
1-inch-wide sheer
   green ribbon
Brown and black ink pads
Black embossing powder
⅛-inch hole punch
Sewing machine with gold
   all-purpose thread
Embossing heat gun
Glue stick

Cut a 9 x 6¼-inch piece of dark green card stock; score and fold in half. Cut a 4½ x 6¼-inch piece of leaf-print paper; trim off upper left corner diagonally. Glue leaf-print paper to card front, lining up bottom and right edges. Machine sew along diagonal edge with a zigzag stitch.

Cut one 1⅞-inch square and one 2⅜-inch squares from pale green card stock.

Attach a butterfly sticker to small square; stamp and emboss "Get Well Soon" onto larger square with black ink and embossing powder.

Layer squares onto beige card stock; trim edges, leaving a small border. Apply brown ink to edges. Machine-stitch around pale green squares. Adhere "Get Well Soon" square to dark green card stock, trimming a ¼-inch border. Punch ⅛-inch holes through corners of "Get Well Soon" square; insert gold brads.

Referring to photo, glue small square in upper left corner of card and larger square in bottom right corner.

Use a craft knife to cut a 1-inch-long slit in center of card fold. Thread ribbon through slit and tie a bow on front of card. Trim ribbon ends.

Use envelope template to cut an envelope from green patterned paper; score and fold lines. Glue side and bottom flaps together.

Repeat process above to make another small butterfly square; glue to envelope flap. ■

SOURCES: Patterned papers from The C-Thru Ruler Co./Déjà Views; stickers and envelope template from Printworks Collection, Inc.; rubber stamp from Stampendous.

Inspiration

Design by CAMI BAUMAN

MATERIALS

Card stock: ivory,
 sage green
Printed paper: floral
 vintage print
7 x 5-inch ivory card
 with envelope
Brown antique-finish
 ink pad
Markers: yellow, sage
 green, purple
Copper metallic rub-on
 cream
Pearlescent acrylic paint:
 white
Air-dry modeling compound
Flower clay mold
¼-inch-wide sheer sage
 green ribbon
Paintbrush
Paper adhesive
Adhesive foam dots
Adhesive dots
Computer font (optional)

To condition modeling compound, knead a small amount with hands until it is a workable consistency. Push compound into flower mold; remove excess compound from edges and back of mold. Remove flower from mold; set aside to dry overnight.

Color flower petals with purple marker; color flower center with yellow marker. Color flower creases with sage green marker. Paint entire flower pearlescent white; let dry.

Cut a 7 x 5-inch piece of printed paper; ink edges. Cut a 4½-inch square from sage green card stock; tear in half diagonally, from corner to corner. Rub copper metallic cream on edges of top half of torn square, including torn edge. Cut a 4½-inch length of ribbon; wrap ribbon diagonally around corner of torn sage green piece; wrap and glue ends to reverse side. Use adhesive dots to attach modeling compound flower to piece, overlapping ribbon.

Cut an 8-inch length of ribbon; lay ribbon across printed paper rectangle, slightly below center. Wrap and glue left ribbon end to reverse side of printed paper. Do not glue opposite end at this time.

Glue the assembled torn piece of sage green card stock with flower on it to upper left corner of printed paper rectangle, lining up straight edges.

Use a computer to generate, or hand-print, "May you find strength in the love that surrounds you." on sage green card stock. Cut a 2¾ x 2½-inch rectangle around sentiment; tear off bottom edge. Rub metallic cream on edges.

Cut a 3⅛ x 2⅝-inch piece of ivory card stock; ink edges. Glue to center of printed paper rectangle without gluing down ribbon. Glue remaining end of ribbon to reverse side of printed paper rectangle. Use adhesive foam dots to attach sentiment rectangle on top of ivory rectangle, overlapping ribbon.

Cut another piece of ribbon and tie a bow; trim ends and glue bow to right side of sentiment rectangle. Glue assembled piece to ivory card.

For envelope, use the top envelope flap of premade envelope as a pattern to trace and cut an envelope flap from printed paper. Ink edges of printed envelope flap. Cut an 8-inch length of ribbon; lay ribbon across printed envelope flap; wrap and glue ends to reverse side. Cut another piece of ribbon and tie a bow; trim ends and glue bow to center of envelope flap. Glue assembled piece to top envelope flap. ∎

SOURCES: Printed paper from K&Company; air-dry modeling compound from Creative Paperclay Co.; ink pad from Ranger; clay mold from Makin's Clay; metallic rub-on cream from Craf-T Products.

For You

Design by SUSAN STRINGFELLOW

Cut a 5½ x 11-inch rectangle from ivory card stock; score and fold in half. Cut a 5¼-inch square from pink card stock; using a sewing machine with no thread, machine-stitch on reverse side of pink square to create a pierced border. Turn square over and lightly sand pierced holes, rub holes with ivory ink. Glue square to card.

Rub tan ink on the edges of a 3 x 4-inch piece of polka-dot paper; glue to upper left corner of card. Glue a piece of turquoise fiber across card along bottom edge of polka-dot paper; trim ends evenly.

Draw a loose shape of a flower petal on a scrap piece of paper; cut petal out and use as a pattern to trace and cut seven petals from pink card stock. **Note:** *Petals do not need to match perfectly.*

Place one petal, face down, onto piercing pad and pierce a swirl design into petal with paper piercing tool. Turn petal over and lightly sand and rub ivory ink on pierced holes. Repeat for each petal. Glue petals onto ivory textured paper, forming a flower.

Cut an uneven circle from polka-dot paper to fit onto center of flower; layer on top of ivory card stock and trim a small border. Attach layered circles to flower center with an ivory brad. Trim a 3-inch square around flower and rub tan ink on edges; glue in lower right corner of card, overlapping fiber. Attach "FOR YOU" letter stickers in upper right corner. ■

SOURCES: Patterned paper and letter stickers from EK Success.

MATERIALS

Pink and ivory card stock
Pink polka-dot print paper
Ivory textured paper
Scrap paper
Turquoise fiber
Metallic letter stickers
Ivory mini round brad
Ivory and tan ink pads
Sandpaper
Piercing pad
Paper piercing tool
Sewing machine
¼-inch hole punch
Glue stick

Picture Perfect

Design by MEREDITH HOLMAN

MATERIALS

- 4¼ x 5½-inch ivory flecked card with envelope
- Light purple card stock
- Pastel striped paper
- 2 white flower tacks
- Flower snapshot sticker
- White slide mount
- ½-inch-wide sheer white polka-dot ribbon
- ⅛-inch hole punch
- Sewing machine with white/pink variegated all-purpose thread
- Glue stick

Cut a 4 x 5¼-inch piece of light purple card stock. Cut a 3¼ x 5-inch piece of striped paper; tear off right vertical edge diagonally. Glue to light purple piece.

Use sewing machine to sew a zigzag stitch along left edge of striped paper piece. Sew a straight stitch along left edge of light purple card stock; attach flower tacks at top and bottom of stitch line. Glue assembled piece to card.

Tie a piece of ribbon around right side of slide mount; attach flower sticker to reverse side of slide mount. Glue to card.

For envelope, glue a 5½ x 4-inch piece of light purple card stock to reverse side of envelope. Cut a 5½ x 1¼-inch strip of striped paper; tear top edge and glue to bottom of light purple piece.

Punch three ⅛-inch holes at bottom of envelope flap; thread ribbon through each hole and tie bows. Trim ribbon ends. ■

SOURCES: Tacks from Chatterbox; sticker from Pebbles Inc.; patterned paper from Doodlebug Design Inc.

Springtime

Design by LORETTA MATEIK

Cut an 8½ x 5½-inch piece of pale green card stock; score and fold in half. Apply purple chalk to the edges of a 4 x 5¼-inch pink card-stock rectangle; center and glue to card.

Glue springtime sentiment onto green card stock; trim edges, leaving a small border. Punch a ⅛-inch hole at bottom of layered sentiment.

Carefully cut out a lilac bunch and stem from embossed paper. Cut the leaves from the stem; set aside. Thread stem through punched hole and glue stem end to the reverse side of sentiment rectangle. Adhere rectangle to card; use adhesive foam dots to attach lilac bunch. Carefully reattach leaves and adhere with glue stick.

Cut out a butterfly from embossed paper; gently bend wings and adhere above sentiment.

Tape butterfly stencil onto light box or light source; lay envelope, face down, on top of stencil. Use stylus to dry emboss butterflies as desired. ∎

SOURCES: Patterned paper from K&Company; sentiment from My Mind's Eye Inc.; stencil from Plaid.

MATERIALS

Card stock: pink, green
  and pale green
Lilac with butterfly
  embossed paper
Springtime sentiment
White envelope to fit a
  4¼ x 5½-inch card
Purple chalk
Butterfly stencil
⅛-inch hole punch
Stylus
Light box or light source
Removable tape
Adhesive foam dots
Glue stick

Musical Thanks

DIAGRAM ON PAGE 152

Design by SUSAN STRINGFELLOW

Cut a 5 x 10-inch piece of dark pink card stock; score and fold in half. Center and glue a 4¾-inch square piece of black card stock to card front.

Cut a 4¾-inch square piece of sheet music print paper; tear off top and bottom edges. Ink edges with black ink. Glue to card, lining up left and right edges with black card stock. Machine-stitch around perimeter of card ¼ inch from edge of black card stock.

Use a computer to generate desired initial, reversed, on reverse side of black card stock; cut out initial with craft knife. **Option:** *Instead of using a computer, use letter template to trace initial on black card stock.* Cut a rectangle around cutout initial, leaving approximately ¾ inch at bottom.

Cut a piece of crackle print paper the same size as initial rectangle; glue to reverse side of initial rectangle, making sure to not apply glue to area of paper that will show through opening. Glue fabric label to lower right corner of rectangle.

Use white chalk ink to stamp "ms." or appropriate title in upper left corner of rectangle. Machine-stitch across the top edge and down right edge of rectangle. Cut a 3-inch length of ribbon; fold in half and trim ends at an angle. Cut a 6-inch length of green fiber; form fiber into three loops and place under paper flower. Place folded end of ribbon underneath green fiber and paper flower; lay assembled piece on lower left corner of initial rectangle. Punch a ¹⁄₁₆-inch hole through flower, fiber, ribbon and rectangle; insert a brad to secure all pieces in place. Cut a 1¼ x 3½-inch rectangle from black mesh; place mesh on left side of card, but do not adhere it to card yet. Glue assembled initial rectangle to card, overlapping mesh.

Cut a 5½-inch length of black wire. Use round-nose pliers to form one end of wire into a tight loop. Slide beads on wire, alternating between seed and bugle beads until 1 inch of wire is left. Holding end of wire and referring to diagram on page 152, form wire into a treble-clef shape. Trim excess wire and form end into a tight loop to secure beads in place. Glue to left side of initial rectangle.

For envelope, use template to trace and cut an envelope from dark pink card stock; score and fold envelope flaps. Glue side and bottom flaps together.

Center and glue a 4¾-inch square piece of sheet music print paper to front of envelope. Cut a 15-inch length of ribbon; wrap ribbon around envelope and knot ends together on the left side. Trim ends. Secure ribbon with paper adhesive. ■

SOURCES: Printed papers from EK Success; label and flower from Making Memories; wire from Artistic Wire; rubber stamps from Hero Arts; chalk ink pad from Tsukineko Inc.; Coluzzle template from Provo Craft.

To My Dear Friend

Design by CHRISTINE TRAVERSA

Score and fold a 5½ x 8½-inch piece of light turquoise card stock in half forming a 5½ x 4¼-inch card. Layer a 5½ x ⅞-inch white card stock strip on top of a 5½ x 1¹⁄₁₆-inch strip of black card stock; center and glue strips to card.

Use a computer or hand print "To my dear friend" onto white card stock; trim a rectangle around words and adhere to black card stock. Trim card stock leaving a small border. Glue rectangle in lower right corner of card.

Place floral stencil on top of floral image; lay on top of light source and emboss image with stylus. Lightly sand image. Trim image leaving a small border; glue onto black card stock and trim a small border. Glue layered image onto card. Punch a ¼-inch circle from black card stock; glue in center of one of the flowers in image.

For envelope, add a floral image to lower left corner. Randomly apply blue ink to edges. ■

SOURCES: Floral image and stencil from Lasting Impressions for Paper Inc.

MATERIALS

Card stock: dark pink, black

Printed papers: pink sheet music, pink crackle

Black mesh

Pink fabric label: "Thanks"

Black craft wire

Beads: clear seed, black bugle

Paper flower

Green fiber

⅜-inch-wide black polka-dot print ribbon

Black mini round brad

Small alphabet rubber stamps

Ink pads: white chalk, black dye

Envelope template to fit a 5-inch square card

Sewing machine with pink all-purpose thread

¹⁄₁₆-inch hole punch

Round-nose pliers

Wire nippers

Paper adhesive

Computer font (optional)

MATERIALS

Card stock: light turquoise, black and white

White envelope to fit a 5½ x 4¼-inch card

Printed floral image with corresponding floral stencil

Blue ink pad

Light box or light source

Sandpaper

Stylus

¼-inch circle punch

Glue stick

Computer font (optional)

Happy Spring

Design by TAMI MAYBERRY

MATERIALS

Blue and white card stock

Blue daisy print paper

Alphabet rub-on transfers

Self-adhesive yellow buttons

Daisy dies with
    die-cutting tool

Light blue ink pad

White envelope to fit
    a 4 x 5⅝-inch card

Stylus

Glue stick

Adhesive foam dots

Cut a 4 x 11¼-inch piece of blue card stock; score and fold in half. Cut a 4 x 2½-inch piece of daisy print paper; tear top edge and glue to bottom of card.

Die-cut two daisies from white card stock; apply light blue ink to edges. Attach adhesive buttons to daisy centers. Use glue stick to attach one daisy in upper left corner; use an adhesive foam dot to attach remaining daisy. Transfer "Happy Spring!" on daisy print paper.

To embellish envelope, apply light blue ink to edges. Cut a 1¾ x 4⅜-inch strip from daisy print paper; tear one long edge and glue along left edge of envelope. ∎

SOURCES: Daisy print paper from Creative Imaginations; daisy die cut and die-cut tool from Sizzix/Ellison; alphabet rub-on transfers from Making Memories and Duncan; self-adhesive buttons from EK Success.

Welcome Little One

Design by JULIE EBERSOLE

Cut a 5½ x 8½-inch piece of white card stock; score and fold in half. Cut a 5¼ x 4-inch piece of pale yellow card stock; punch a 1⅜-inch square toward upper left corner.

Use black ink to stamp pacifier image onto white card stock; color with markers and punch a 1¼-inch square around image. Layer onto a 1⅜-inch square punched from pink card stock. Punch a ⅛-inch hole in one of the corners. Thread ribbons through hole and through punched square in pale yellow card stock. Tie into a bow and trim ends. Glue assembled piece onto card; secure pacifier square with glue.

Cut a 5¼ x 1-inch strip from polka-dot paper; stamp sentiment onto strip with black ink. Glue across bottom of card.

Use envelope template as a guide to cut a piece of pale yellow circles print paper to fit inside premade white envelope. Glue piece inside envelope.

Use pale yellow, pale pink and pale peach ink pads to stamp solid circles across bottom front of envelope. ∎

SOURCE: Rubber stamps, punches, envelope, envelope template and patterned papers from Stampin' Up!.

MATERIALS

Card stock: pale yellow, pink and white
Patterned papers: white polka dots, pale yellow circles
White envelope to fit a 5½ x 4¼-inch card
Envelope template to fit a 5½ x 4¼-inch card
Rubber stamps: solid circle, "sentiment" and pacifier
Ink pads: black, pale yellow, pale pink and pale peach
Markers: pale yellow, pale pink and pale blue
¼-inch-wide pink gingham ribbon
⅜-inch-wide pale pink organdy ribbon
1¼- and 1⅜-inch square punches
⅛-inch hole punch
Glue stick

Baby Announcement

Design by HEATHER D. WHITE

Lightly ink edges and surface, inside and out, of premade card. Cut a piece of polka-dot print paper slightly smaller than card front; ink edges. Center and glue to card.

Open card and use a craft knife to carefully cut out window opening on card front. Cut a 2⅛ x 2-inch rectangle from paisley print paper; ink edges. Center and glue rectangle over opening on card front. Open card and use a craft knife to carefully cut out window opening on card front. Ink inside edges of opening.

With stripes vertical, cut a 3⅞ x 3-inch rectangle from striped paper; tear off long edges. Ink edges. Glue piece to card below window opening. Transfer "oh, baby" rub-on to center of torn piece.

Cut a 5-inch piece of ribbon in half; knot ends together and attach to bottom portion of card with double-sided tape. Trim ends if needed.

Using a computer and scanner, scan baby photo. With scanned image toward top portion of computer screen, begin to layout desired birth announcement information. Print out information on a piece of computer printer paper to determine correct size and placement of photo. Photo needs to show through window opening of card. Once size and placement has been determined, print final copy on the reverse side of harlequin print paper for an ivory background. *Option: Instead of scanning photo, make photo copies and instead of laying out text on computer, hand–write announcement information.* If desired, transfer "simply adorable" at top of birth announcement information. Cut information to fit inside card; ink edges and glue to card.

For envelope, take apart premade envelope and use as a template to trace and cut an envelope from paisley print paper. Score and fold envelope flaps; ink edges and surface. Use double-sided tape to secure side and bottom flaps together.

Cut a 3⁵⁄₁₆ x 9⁷⁄₁₆-inch piece of polka-dot print paper; ink edges. Center and glue to front of envelope. Cut a 2¹¹⁄₁₆ x 9⁷⁄₁₆-inch piece of harlequin print paper; turn paper over and ink edges and surface. With ivory side face up, glue to front of envelope on top of polka-dot paper. Cut a 5-inch piece of ribbon in half; knot ends together. Use double-sided tape to attach ribbon to bottom portion of envelope on top of layered papers. Trim ribbon ends if needed. ∎

SOURCES: Card, printed papers and ribbon from Making Memories; rub-on transfers from The C-Thru Ruler Co.

MATERIALS

Premade 3⅞ x 9¼-inch
    card with window
    opening
Matching envelope
Coordinating printed
    papers: brown polka
    dot, cream blue/brown
    paisley print, blue/
    brown striped, brown/
    ivory harlequin print
⅝-inch-wide blue/brown
    striped ribbon
Rub-on transfers:
    "oh, baby,"
    "simply adorable"
Brown dye ink pad
Craft knife
Double-sided tape
Glue stick
Computer, scanner and
    computer printer
    paper (optional)

MATERIALS

Clear vellum

Metallic gold and
   turquoise card stock

Canning lid

Envelope to fit a 5⅜ x
   4½-inch card

Vintage angel image

Filigree frame stamp

Light blue grosgrain ribbon

Ultrafine glitter

Ultra-thick embossing
   enamel or clear
   dimensional adhesive

Gold and clear embossing
   powders

Ink pads: black solvent-
   based, watermark and
   metallic gold

Ivory acrylic paint

Sandpaper

Paintbrush

Needle-nose pliers

Awl

Heat gun

Craft glue

Birth Announcement

Design by KIMBERLY KWAN

ALTERED CANNING LID

Use needle-nose pliers to crimp the edges of the standard sealing disk from the canning lid (the part without the threading). Use an awl to poke a hole on the left and right sides of lid. Sand shiny metal portion of lid; rub black ink on crimped edges.

Paint top of lid ivory; let dry partially for a minute and wipe some paint off. When dry, apply watermark ink to top of lid and sprinkle on a liberal amount of embossing enamel; heat with heat gun and repeat for two to three layers.

Adhere angel image to lid with a small dot of craft glue. Repeat embossing enamel process until a thick, resin-like coat covers image. Add a small amount of ultrafine glitter through-out layers, if desired.

CARD

Cut an 11 x 4½-inch piece of metallic gold card stock; score and fold a line 2¾ inches from right edges and another line 2¾ inches from left edge, creating a bifold card.

Stamp filigree frame image onto turquoise card stock with watermark ink; sprinkle with clear embossing powder and heat. Cut a rectangle around frame and layer onto clear vellum; trim edges, leaving a small border. Apply watermark ink to edges of vellum; emboss with gold embossing powder.

Cut layered piece in half; close card and glue one half to left side of opening and other half to right side, lining up edges of frame so they match when card is closed.

Thread grosgrain ribbon through holes in altered canning lid; adhere left back side of canning lid to left side of card opening. Refer to photo for placement. Wrap ribbon around card and tie into a bow. Trim ribbon ends. Untie bow and glue ribbon on back of card to secure. Cut a small circle from turquoise card stock; adhere to back of canning lid to help hide ribbon.

Use a computer font or hand print birth announcement onto clear vellum; trim a rectangle around announcement. Adhere inside card.

ENVELOPE

Carefully disassemble premade envelope; use as a template to trace and cut an envelope from turquoise card stock. Score and fold lines.

Trace inside of envelope and envelope flap onto metallic gold card stock; cut out and adhere inside envelope. Adhere a piece of metallic gold card stock to outside of envelope flap. ∎

SOURCES: Filigree frame stamp from Magenta; ink pads from Tsukineko Inc.

It's a Girl

Design by BARBARA GREVE

Cut a 5 x 6½-inch piece of pink gingham print vellum; place on front of card and punch two ¼-inch holes at center top. Thread pink gingham ribbon through holes and tie a bow. Trim ribbon ends.

Cut two clear vellum rectangles, one measuring 3¾ x 1⅛ inches and the other 4 x 1⅛ inches. Transfer "It's A Girl" onto rectangles, using alphabet rub-ons. Cut two rectangles from pink vellum, one measuring 2¾ x 1 inches and the other 3 x 1 inches. Referring to photo, glue pink rectangles toward center of card; lay clear vellum rectangles on top of pink rectangles. Use sewing needle and white embroidery floss to sew a baby-themed button at each end of clear vellum rectangles. Tie knots on front of buttons and secure with gem adhesive. ∎

SOURCES: Buttons from Doodlebug Design Inc.; alphabet rub-on transfers from Making Memories; Gem-Tac adhesive from Beacon.

MATERIALS

5 x 6½-inch blank card
Vellum: pink gingham print, clear, pink
White alphabet rub-on transfers
Pink gingham ribbon
4 baby-themed buttons
White embroidery floss
¼-inch hole punch
Sewing needle
Vellum tape
Gem adhesive

Bundle of Joy

Design by MARY AYRES

MATERIALS

Card stock: white, light
yellow and yellow

White envelope to fit an
8 x 5-inch card

4 pewter round brads

2 round button snaps

2-inch square black
slide mounts

Color copy of a baby photo
plus 6 black-and-white
wallet-size copies

White craft thread

1/16- and 1/8-inch
circle punches

Sewing machine with black
all-purpose thread

Instant-dry paper adhesive

Computer font (optional)

Score and fold an 8 x 10-inch piece of light yellow card stock in half to form an 8 x 5-inch card. Trim a 7½ x 4½-inch rectangle from white card stock. Cut black-and-white photocopies into the following measurements: 2 x 2⅜ inches, 3¼ x 2⅜ inches, 1¾ x 2⅜ inches, 2 x 1⅝ inches, 3¼ x 1⅝ inches and 1¾ x 1⅝ inches. Arrange and glue photos onto white rectangle, leaving ⅛ inch between each photo.

Machine stitch across lengths and widths of photos ⅛ inch from edges; glue thread ends on reverse side of rectangle. Glue rectangle to card.

To create window opening, cut a 7 x 2¾-inch piece of yellow card stock. Score and fold a line 1¾ inches from left edge and another line 1¾ inches from right edge, creating two flaps. Cut four 1¼ x 2¼-inch rectangles from light yellow card stock. Glue two rectangles onto the two front panels; machine stitch ⅛ inch from edges of light yellow rectangles. Glue remaining light yellow rectangles inside panels to cover.

Punch a ⅛-inch hole in the center of both front panels; attach button snaps. Glue a 3¼ x 2½-inch color photo inside opening. Glue assembled piece toward upper left corner of card. Close doors and tie white craft thread around button snaps and into a bow.

Use a computer or hand print "a baby is a bundle of joy" onto white card stock; trim a rectangle around words and glue on reverse side of slide mount. Punch 1/16-inch holes at center top and bottom of slide mount; attach pewter brads. Glue slide mount in bottom right corner. Repeat process to create another slide mount; glue to envelope flap. ■

SOURCES: Button snaps from Cloud 9 Design; slide mounts from Design Originals; Zip Dry paper adhesive from Beacon.

Oh, Baby

Design by CAMI BAUMAN

Cut a 7 x 10-inch piece of white card stock; score and fold in half. Die-cut a square from orange card stock; trim a 6½ x 4⅜-inch rectangle from yellow card stock. Machine stitch orange square at center top of yellow rectangle using a zigzag stitch. Attach duck sticker to square; transfer "oh, baby" below square. Place photo corners on yellow rectangle and glue to card. ■

SOURCES: Sticker from Marcel Schurman Creations; rub-on transfer from The C-Thru Ruler Co./Déjà Views; square die and die-cutting tool from Sizzix/Ellison.

MATERIALS

Card stock: white, yellow and orange
Embellished duck sticker
"oh, baby" rub-on transfer
Black photo corners
Square die with die cutting tool
Sewing machine with white all-purpose thread
Glue stick

She's Here!

Design by JULIE EBERSOLE

Cut an 8½ x 5½-inch piece of white card stock; score and fold in half. Cut a 4 x 5¼-inch piece of pale yellow card stock; glue to card. Glue a 4 x ¾-inch strip of striped paper across pale yellow card stock slightly below center. Punch three ⅛-inch holes on right side of strip; set eyelets. Glue piece to card.

Punch a 1¼-inch circle from striped paper; glue to reverse side of tag. Glue button to front of tag; draw a mouth and a tiny hair curl on button with marker.

Stamp "she's here" below button with black solvent-based ink. Punch a ⅛-inch hole at top of tag; thread ribbon through and tie a knot. Trim ends. Glue tag to card.

Use envelope template to trace and cut an envelope from pink vellum; score and fold lines. Glue side and bottom flaps together. ■

SOURCES: Rubber stamp, striped paper, tag, circle punch and envelope template from Stampin' Up!.

MATERIALS

Pale yellow and white card stock
Pink striped paper
Pink vellum
Envelope template to fit a 4¼ x 5½-inch card
"she's here" rubber stamp
Black solvent-based ink pad
Black fine-tip permanent marker
Metal-edge vellum tag
Pink button
Pink eyelets with eyelet setter tool
¼-inch-wide pink gingham ribbon
1¼-inch circle punch
⅛-inch hole punch
Adhesive foam squares
Paper adhesive

It's a Shower!

Design by JULIE EBERSOLE

MATERIALS

Blue striped paper

Card stock: pale yellow, white, lavender

Rubber stamps: alphabet circles, "It's a Party," safety pin square and "oh baby" text background

Ink pads: watermark and purple dye ink

Clear embossing powder

Silver eyelet with eyelet setter tool

Silver metallic cord

Embossing heat gun

Craft sponge

1/16-inch hole punch

Glue stick

Score and fold an 8½ x 5½-inch piece of pale yellow card stock in half, forming a 4¼ x 5½-inch card. Glue a 3⅞ x 5⅛-inch piece of striped paper to card.

Use purple ink to stamp "oh baby" text background onto white card stock; use watermark ink to stamp safety pin image on top of text. Emboss safety pin image with clear embossing powder. Lightly sponge purple ink around and on top of safety pin; trim a 1¾ x 2½-inch rectangle around image. Glue onto pale yellow card stock.

Trim pale yellow card stock into a tag shape. Cut a ⅝ x 2¾-inch strip of lavender card stock; fold in half and secure unfolded end at top of tag with silver eyelet.

Stamp "It's a" onto pale yellow card stock with purple ink; cut out "It's a" party words and punch a 1/16-inch hole at top corner. Punch a 1/16-inch hole in card fold toward top left corner. Thread silver cord through hole and thread on "It's a" and safety-pin tag; tie a knot and trim ends.

Use alphabet circles to stamp "shower" vertically down right side of card with purple ink. Secure tag and words with glue. ■

SOURCES: Text background stamp from A Muse Artstamps; all other stamps from Stampin' Up!; watermark ink pad from Tsukineko Inc.

Just Ducky

Design by JULIE EBERSOLE

Cut a 5½ x 8½-inch piece of pale blue card stock; score and fold in half. Use pale blue chalk-finish ink to stamp front of card randomly with solid circles. Trim bottom front edge with decorative-edge scissors.

Stamp long oval onto white card stock with light blue ink; stamp "just ducky!" directly beneath oval with black ink. Trim a 3½ x 1½-inch rectangle around oval and words. Mount to pale yellow card stock; trim edges, leaving a small border. Glue to card.

Punch three ducks from pale yellow card stock; mount to pale blue oval with foam dots. Wrap ribbon through card; tie a knot in front and trim ends.

Use envelope template to trace and cut an envelope from white polka-dot paper; score and fold lines. Glue side and bottom flaps together. ∎

SOURCES: Rubber stamps from A Muse Artstamps; punch from EK Success; polka-dot paper and envelope template from Stampin Up!.

MATERIALS

Card stock: pale blue, white and pale yellow
White polka-dot print paper
Rubber stamps: solid circle, long oval and "just ducky!"
Pale blue chalk-finish ink pad
Light blue and black ink pads
Duck punch
⅜-inch-wide white organdy ribbon
Decorative-edge scissors
Envelope template to fit a 5½ x 4¼-inch card
Adhesive foam dots
Glue stick

Special Delivery

Design by JULIE EBERSOLE

Stamp abstract shape onto white card stock with pale blue ink; stamp stork on top of shape with black ink. Trim a rectangle around images and layer onto blue card stock; trim edges forming a tag shape.

Fold top portion of tag over top edge of white card stock; set three eyelets to secure. Glue tag onto note card. Stamp "special delivery" underneath image with black ink.

Use pale blue ink to stamp circle outline, heart, postal cancellation mark and "special delivery" in top right corner of envelope. ∎

SOURCES: Rubber stamps from A Muse Artstamps and Plaid/All Night Media.

MATERIALS

White and blue card stock
Rubber stamps: abstract shape, stork, "special delivery," small heart, circle outline and postal cancellation mark
Black and pale blue ink pads
White eyelets with eyelet setter tool
Raised-edge note card with envelope
Glue stick

Baby Carriage

Designs by KATHLEEN PANEITZ

MATERIALS

12 x 12-inch dusty blue harlequin print paper
Light green patterned paper
White card stock
Self-adhesive quilled baby boy carriage embellishment
Envelope template to fit a 5 x 4½-inch card
"cherish" light blue printed ribbon
"sweet baby boy" blue printed twill ribbon
Dusty blue ink pad
Glue stick
Adhesive dots

Cut a 10 x 4½-inch piece of white card stock; score and fold in half. Cut a piece of dusty blue harlequin print paper slightly smaller than card front. Apply dusty blue ink to the edges of a 2¼ x 3¼-inch light green patterned rectangle; layer onto white card stock. Trim edges, leaving a small border. Glue to harlequin print paper.

Wrap a piece of "sweet baby boy" printed ribbon across bottom of paper; adhere ribbon ends on reverse side. Attach quilled baby carriage onto layered rectangles, overlapping ribbon. Tie a bow with "cherish" ribbon; use an adhesive dot to attach bow in upper left corner. Glue assembled piece to card.

Use envelope template to trace and cut an envelope from harlequin print paper; score and fold lines. Glue side and bottom flaps together. ◼

SOURCES: Patterned papers from K&Company and Creative Imaginations; carriage quilled sticker from EK Success; "cherish" ribbon from Making Memories; "sweet baby boy" ribbon from Creative Impressions; envelope template from The C-Thru Ruler Co.

Baby Thank You

Design by CHRIS NIEMEIER

MATERIALS

Pale pink card stock
Baby footprints and "Thank You Very Much!" rubber stamps
Pink and light pink ink pads
Decorative-edge ruler
Stylus
Clear glitter glue

Score and fold a 5½ x 8½-inch piece of pale pink card stock in half, forming a 5½ x 4¼-inch card. Use light pink ink to stamp baby footprints on center of card front. Use pink ink to stamp sentiment below footprints.

Open card and position decorative-edge ruler toward bottom of card front; use stylus to dry emboss a line along decorative edge. Close card and add a wavy line of clear glitter glue below stamped sentiment. ◼

SOURCES: Baby footprints rubber stamp from Hero Arts; sentiment rubber stamp from Plaid/All Night Media; decorative-edge ruler from Art Deckle.

Baby, Baby, Baby

Design by CAMI BAUMAN

Cut a 10 x 7-inch piece of white card stock; score and fold in half. Adhere a 5 x 7-inch piece of pink card stock to card; adhere a 4¾ x 6¾-inch piece of pink striped paper on top.

Attach baby buggy sticker to orange card stock; trim a rectangle around sticker. Layer rectangle onto white and pink card stocks, trimming small borders.

Cut a 4¾-inch piece of twill ribbon; using orange ink pad, stamp "Baby Baby Baby" onto twill. Adhere to pink card stock. Trim a small border on top and bottom; trim side ends even with ribbon. Glue to card approximately 1 inch from bottom edge.

To embellish envelope, cover envelope flap with pink striped paper; trim edges even. Glue a 2½ x ⅞-inch orange card-stock rectangle to pink card stock. Trim a small border and glue to flap, extending out from bottom edge. ∎

SOURCES: Striped paper from KI Memories; sticker from Scrap-Ease; alphabet stamps from Duncan.

MATERIALS

Card stock: orange, pink and white
Pink striped paper
White envelope to fit a 5 x 7-inch card
Silver baby buggy sticker
Alphabet stamps
Orange ink pad
Twill ribbon
Glue stick

MATERIALS

Card stock: white, blue,
    pink and light purple
Light pink crinkle and blue
    striped patterned papers
Pink and blue envelopes to
    fit 7 x 5-inch cards
16 silver round mini brads
4 (⅛-inch) silver
    round eyelets
¼-inch-wide pink
    satin ribbon
¼-inch-wide blue
    satin ribbon
Pink and blue buttons
Baby girl and baby boy
    themed stickers: diaper
    pins, rattles, pacifiers
    and shoes
Ink pads: purple, pink
    and blue
Circle punches: 1¼-inch,
    ¹⁄₁₆-inch and ⅛-inch
Computer font (optional)
Sewing machine with white
    all-purpose thread
Permanent fabric adhesive
Paper adhesive

Baby Boy & Baby Girl

Design by MARY AYRES

Project note: Use all blue papers and embellishments for boy card; use all pink papers and embellishments for girl card.

Cut a 7 x 10-inch piece of white card stock; score and fold in half. Cut a 3½ x 1½-inch rectangle from pink or blue patterned paper; rub matching ink on edges and glue in upper left corner of card. Cut a 3½ x 2¾-inch rectangle from light purple card stock; rub purple ink on edges and glue in lower left corner.

Cut a 2¾ x 2¼-inch rectangle from light purple card stock; rub edges with purple ink and glue in upper right corner. Cut a 2¼ x 1¾-inch rectangle from white card stock; rub pink or blue ink on edges and glue onto light purple rectangle.

Use a computer or hand print "A baby girl (boy) is a dream come true" onto pink or blue patterned paper; trim a 2¾ x 2-inch rectangle around words. Rub matching ink on edges and glue in lower right corner.

Machine stitch around light purple rectangles ⅛ inch from edges. Cut a 2¼ x 1½-inch rectangle from pink or blue card stock; rub purple ink on edges. Place rectangle on patterned rectangle in lower right corner and machine stitch ⅛ inch from left edge. Bend rectangle along stitched line to open.

Punch a 1¼-inch circle from purple card stock; rub edges with purple ink. Glue circle to pink (blue) rectangle; glue pink (blue) button to circle.

Referring to photo, attach baby-themed stickers in remaining squares. Punch ⅛-inch holes on both sides of pacifier sticker; attach eyelets. Insert ribbon through eyelets and tie a knot. Trim ribbon ends. Make two ribbon ties; trim ends and glue to baby shoes.

Punch ¹⁄₁₆-inch holes in the corners of patterned paper rectangles; attach brads.

For envelope, trim a 4 x 1¾-inch rectangle from purple card stock. Rub purple ink on edges and glue to envelope flap. Attach baby rattle sticker to rectangle. Machine stitch around rectangle ⅛ inch from edges. Make a ribbon tie; trim ends and glue to rattle. ∎

SOURCES: Patterned papers from K&Company and Creative Imaginations; stickers from Frances Meyer Inc.; Fabri-Tac permanent adhesive from Beacon.

A New Arrival

Design by ANGELIA WIGGINTON

MATERIALS

4¼ x 5½-inch polka-
dot card
4¼ x 5½-inch pink
printed card
Ivory envelope to fit a
4¼ x 5½-inch card
Self-adhesive acrylic "a
new arrival" sticker
"A new arrival" sticker
Pink scrapbook buckle
Pink mini brads
Light pink cotton fabric
Sandpaper
Craft knife
Glue stick

Cut polka-dot card in half at the fold. Lightly sand inside and outside surfaces of pink card; lightly sand polka-dot piece. Use a craft knife to cut a 1¾ x 1-inch rectangle in lower right corner on front of pink card. Attach the acrylic sticker inside card showing through rectangle.

Fray the edges of a 1¼ x 14-inch piece of pink fabric; wrap fabric around front of pink card. Thread each end through the buckle and secure ends with mini brads. Trim fabric ends.

Attach sticker to upper left corner of polka-dot piece; insert mini brads on each end of sticker. Glue polka-dot piece to front of envelope. ■

SOURCES: Cards, envelope and stickers from K&Company; buckle from Junkitz.

Baby Welcome

Design by ANGELIA WIGGINTON

MATERIALS

Premade tag-shape card
with envelope
Acrylic baby-theme stickers
Baby-theme stickers
Coordinating striped paper
Floral frame rub-on transfer
Light pink cotton fabric
White lace
Sandpaper
Adhesive foam dots
Glue stick

Lightly sand tag card; attach acrylic sticker in lower right corner with an adhesive foam dot. Thread pink fabric through holes in tag and tie a bow. Thread lace through baby-theme sticker tag; tie through holes into a bow.

Cover envelope flap with striped paper; sand edges. Attach a sticker with adhesive foam dot. Transfer floral frame rub-on to front of envelope; attach sticker in lower left corner. ■

SOURCES: Card, envelope, stickers, rub-on transfer and striped paper from K&Company.

Baby Blessings

Design by KATHLEEN PANEITZ

Cut a 6½ x 7¾-inch piece of white card stock; score and fold in half. Referring to photo, trim a piece of floral print stitched paper slightly smaller than card front. Stamp baby sentiment in top portion of stitched paper; attach a mini flower brad through each printed flower. Cut a piece of ribbon; staple in lower right corner. Glue assembled piece to card.

Use template to trace and cut an envelope from striped paper; score and fold lines. Glue side and bottom flaps together. ***Note:*** *Width and height of template measurements may need to be adjusted slightly to fit card.* ∎

SOURCES: Stitched paper from Autumn Leaves; floral print paper from Scrapbook Wizard; rubber stamp from Duncan; mini flower brads from Making Memories; printed ribbon from Creative Impressions; envelope template from The C-Thru Ruler Co.

MATERIALS

Pink/cream floral print
   stitched paper
Pink striped paper
White card stock
Envelope template to fit
   a 6½ x 3⅞-inch card
Baby sentiment stamp
Black ink pad
Silver mini flower brads
Pink "sweet baby girl"
   print ribbon
Stapler with staples
Glue stick

A Baby Is a Blessing

Design by CHRIS NIEMEIER

Cut a 5½ x 8½-inch piece of white textured card stock; score and fold in half. Use a computer to generate, or hand print desired birth information inside card.

Cut a 4⅞ x 3⅝-inch piece of glossy white card stock; use light blue ink to stamp clouds onto piece. Let dry. Layer onto light yellow card stock; trim edges, leaving a small border. Wrap ribbon around left side of layered rectangles; tie a knot and trim ends. Glue to card.

Use watermark ink to stamp baby sentiment onto smooth white card stock; emboss with silver embossing powder. Trim a rectangle around sentiment and layer onto light yellow card stock. Trim a small border. Color in stars with yellow marker. Center and glue to card. ∎

SOURCES: Watermark ink pad from Tsukineko Inc.; sentiment rubber stamp from Duncan; clouds rubber stamp from Mostly Animals.

MATERIALS

Card stock: light yellow,
   smooth white, glossy
   white and white
   textured
Clouds and baby sentiment
   rubber stamps
⅝-inch-wide sheer
   yellow ribbon
Silver embossing powder
Watermark and light blue
   ink pads
Yellow marker
Embossing heat gun
Glue stick
Computer font (optional)

Baby Blocks

Design by SHARON REINHART

MATERIALS

Blue card stock
Blue square patterned
  paper
White envelope to fit a
  5½ x 4¼-inch card
Baby rattle brass template
Clear dimensional
  square stickers
Alphabet stamps
Light blue ink pad
White metallic
  rub-on cream
Blue domed button
Button shank remover
Embossing stylus
Bone folder
Light box or light source
Removable tape
Adhesive dots
Glue stick

Cut a 5½ x 8½-inch piece of blue card stock; score and fold in half. Use removable tape to attach brass template to front of card; turn card over and place on light box or light source, sandwiching template between light and card stock. Open card and trace design with stylus, pressing card stock into edge of template. Remove tape. Rub white metallic cream on embossed design.

Trim a 3¼ x 4¾-inch piece of blue patterned paper. Stamp letters for "Baby Boy" into squares, beginning in upper left corner and working down. Glue toward left side of card; fold excess paper over top edge. Attach six clear stickers on top of desired section of letters.

To embellish envelope, trim a 3¼ x 2-inch rectangle from blue patterned paper; cut both left corners diagonally to form a tag. Stamp letters of baby's name in squares; adhere to envelope. ***Note:** Make a larger tag if there are not enough squares to accommodate desired name.* Remove shank from button; use an adhesive dot to attach button to left end of tag. ■

SOURCES: Patterned paper from Ivy Cottage Creations; template and stylus from Lasting Impressions for Paper Inc.; clear square stickers from K&Company; alphabet rubber stamps from Plaid/All Night Media; metallic rub-on cream from Craf-T Products.

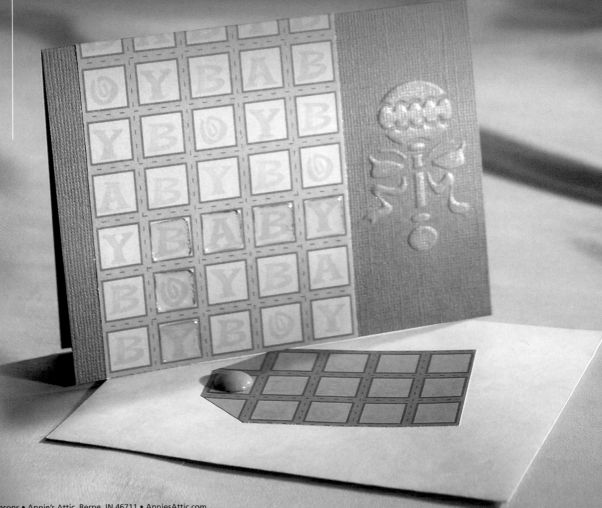

Amazed by You

Design by KATHLEEN PANIETZ

Cut a 5¼ x 10¾-inch rectangle from pink card stock; score a line 2⅞ inches from top and another line 4 inches from bottom. Fold scored lines with top flap overlapping bottom flap.

Choose a few embossed stickers and attach each to cream card stock. Trim rectangles around stickers and ink edges. Glue rectangles to top flap. Embellish top flap with any remaining desired stickers. Attach a border strip sticker along bottom edge of top flap.

Adhere twill ribbon in lower right corner on bottom flap. Attach alphabet stickers to cream card stock, spelling "mom." Apply light green ink to edges. Glue letters in lower left corner of bottom flap.

Use envelope template to trace and cut an envelope from floral print paper; score and fold lines. Glue side and bottom flaps together. ■

SOURCES: Embossed stickers and patterned paper from K&Company; ribbon from Creative Impressions; alphabet stickers from Creative Imaginations; envelope template from The C-Thru Ruler Co.

MATERIALS

Pink and cream card stock
Peach floral print paper
Embossed floral print
  stickers
Envelope template to fit a
  5¼ x 4-inch card
"I am amazed by YOU"
  printed twill ribbon
Light green alphabet
  stickers
Light green ink pad
Stylus
Glue stick

A New Angle on Love

Design by L I N D A B E E S O N

MATERIALS

Card and envelope
   template
Card stock: white, purple,
   dark green and green
Double-sided green
   patterned paper
Double-sided green floral
   print paper
Pansy vellum stickers
Black letter stickers
Decorative nail head
Glue stick

Use card template to trace and cut a card from double-sided green floral print paper. Do not cut out triangle window opening. Score and fold. Cut a dark green triangle slightly larger than triangle opening in template; layer a slightly smaller green triangle on top.

Attach a pansy sticker to white card stock; trim a triangle around sticker. Layer onto purple card stock; trim edges, leaving a small border. Glue on top of layered green triangles.

Trim approximately a 1½ x ¾-inch rectangle from green patterned paper; cut top two corners off diagonally, forming a tag. Place "mom" letter stickers on tag; attach to lower left corner of layered triangles with nail head. Glue triangles to card.

Use envelope template to trace and cut an envelope from green patterned paper; do not cut small triangle opening on envelope flap. Score and fold lines; glue side and bottom flaps together.

Use template to cut a triangle for envelope flap from purple card stock; layer a green floral print triangle cut slightly smaller on top. Attach a pansy sticker to white card stock; trim a small triangle around sticker and layer onto green card stock. Trim edges, leaving a small border. ∎

SOURCES: Card and envelope templates from Wordsworth; green patterned papers from Bo-Bunny Press; vellum stickers from Printworks; letter stickers from Mrs. Grossman's; nail head from Jewel Craft.

Wonderful Mother

Design by TAMI MAYBERRY

MATERIALS

Card stock: burgundy,
   green and burgundy/
   pink double-sided
Coordinating patterned
   paper
Transparency
Envelope template to fit
   an 8 x 5-inch card
"Mom" fabric tag
"happiness" twill ribbon
⅝-inch-wide sheer
   burgundy ribbon
Burgundy button
Burgundy silk flower
Burgundy embroidery
   thread
Mini brad
Mother-themed word
   rub-on transfers
Metal flower charm
Green acrylic paint
Heart confetti
Silver seed beads
White glitter flakes
Light brown ink pad
Sewing needle
Stylus
Steel ruler
Sandpaper
Craft knife
Paintbrush
Mini adhesive dots
½-inch-wide adhesive
   foam tape
½-inch-wide double-stick
   tape

Score and fold an 8 x 10-inch piece of burgundy card stock in half, forming an 8 x 5-inch card. Cut a 2 x 3¼-inch rectangle from burgundy/pink double-sided card stock; sand lightly on burgundy side. Glue in lower right corner at an angle, leaving lower right corner unattached.

Cut a 5⅜ x 4¼-inch rectangle from patterned paper; glue to left side of card at an angle, overlapping sanded burgundy rectangle. Leave lower left corner unattached.

To create shaker box, cut a 4¼ x 3-inch rectangle from double-sided card stock. Use craft knife and steel ruler to cut an "X" in rectangle, from corner to corner, stopping ½ inch from edges.

Apply ½-inch-wide double-stick tape along the outside edge on the burgundy side. Cut a 4¼ x 2¾-inch piece of transparency and place on burgundy side. Apply ½-inch-wide foam tape along outside edges of burgundy side.

Turn piece over and begin folding back the card-stock flaps, exposing the burgundy side. Make sure to stop at the edge of the foam tape. Fold each side inward again, lining up folds with outside edges; fold outward one more time. Use mini adhesive dots to secure folds.

Lightly sand frame. Cut a 4¾ x 3½-inch rectangle from green card stock; tear edges. Transfer desired quote onto center of green card stock. Fill shaker box with seed beads, glitter flakes and confetti. Adhere green card stock to back and seal. Apply brown ink to edges of green card stock. Paint flower charm; let dry and attach to bottom center of frame with an adhesive dot. Glue frame to card.

Wrap a piece of sheer ribbon across bottom of card, wrapping ends of ribbon around papers. Secure ribbon ends and papers with adhesive dots. Glue "mom" tag to sanded burgundy card stock; attach silk flower at left end of ribbon with a brad. Sew button with red thread; tie a knot and trim ends. Glue button to card. Glue "happiness" twill ribbon in lower right corner. Transfer desired words randomly to card.

For envelope, use template to trace and cut an envelope from patterned paper. ***Note: Extend width 1 inch.*** Score and fold lines; glue side and bottom flaps together. Transfer desired mother's day sentiment in bottom left corner. ■

SOURCES: Double-sided card stock from Paper Adventures; patterned paper from Magenta; "mom" tag from Junkitz; "happiness" twill ribbon from Making Memories; word rub-on transfers from Royal & Langnickel; Coluzzle envelope template from Provo Craft.

Mom of the Year

Design by MARY AYRES

MATERIALS

Card stock: white, blue,
     red and yellow
White envelope to fit a
     5½-inch square card
Mother sentiment
     rub-on transfers
Round brads: 3 red,
     3 blue and 5 yellow
Blue ink pad
¹⁄₁₆-inch round anywhere
     punch
Instant-dry paper adhesive

Cut a 5½ x 11-inch piece of white card stock; score and fold in half. Cut three 1½-inch squares from blue card stock, three 1½-inch squares from red card stock and three 1½-inch squares from yellow card stock. Ink edges of each square. Score a line ³⁄₈ inch from top edge on each square.

Referring to photo, position squares on card leaving ¼ inch between each square. Glue top edges of squares to card. Punch a ¹⁄₁₆-inch hole at top of each square; attach red brads to blue squares, yellow brads to red squares and blue brads to yellow squares.

Transfer "Happy Mom's Day" to the three red squares; transfer a mother-themed word underneath each square.

For envelope, trim a 1 x 5½-inch rectangle from red card stock; ink edges. Transfer "MOM OF THE YEAR" to strip. Punch a ¹⁄₁₆-inch hole at each end; attach remaining yellow brads. Glue along left edge of envelope. ∎

SOURCES: Rub-on transfers from Royal & Langnickel; Zip Dry paper adhesive from Beacon

Flower Basket

Design by KATHLEEN PANEITZ

Cut a 5½ x 8½-inch piece of white card stock; score and fold in half. Cover card front with striped paper; trim edges even with card.

Cut a piece of white card stock slightly larger than quilled flower basket; apply brown ink to edges. Tie ribbon around inked card stock; tie a bow and trim ends diagonally. Mat tied rectangle onto pink card stock; trim edges, leaving a small border. Attach quilled flower basket; glue to right side of card.

Transfer rub-on letters to spell "Happy Mother's Day" on left side of card.

To embellish envelope, cut a 2-inch-wide strip of striped paper; glue along left edge. Transfer "Mother's Day 2005" onto strip. ∎

SOURCES: Patterned paper from KI Memories; flower basket quilled sticker from EK Success; rub-on transfers from Li'l Davis Designs and Autumn Leaves.

MATERIALS

Striped paper
Pink and white card stock
White envelope to fit a
    5½ x 4¼-inch card
Self-adhesive quilled
    flower basket
    embellishment
Brown ink pad
Pink rectangle alphabet
    rub-on transfers
Alphabet and number
    rub-on transfers
⅝-inch-wide sheer
    pink ribbon
Glue stick

A Mother's Love

Design by KATHLEEN PANEITZ

MATERIALS

Pink striped paper

Card stock: white, pale green and pink

White envelope to fit a 5½ x 4¼-inch card

Black and pale green ink pads

Alphabet stamps

"Happy Mother's Day" stamp

Pink and white paper flowers

Off-white photo anchor

Definitions: "precious" and "enduring"

Black alphabet rub-on transfers

Pink daisy rub-on transfer

Silver jump ring

Pink mini brad

Pink button

⅜-inch-wide green sheer polka-dot ribbon

"a mother's LOVE" printed green ribbon

Clear pressed daisy sticker

Small love sentiment silver charm

Green floss

Sewing needle

Stylus

Paper adhesive

Computer font (optional)

Cut a 5½ x 8½-inch piece of white card stock; score and fold in half. Cut a 5½ x 4¼-inch piece of pink striped paper. Wrap a piece of printed ribbon across paper; adhere ends on reverse side.

Cut a 1¾ x 6-inch strip of pale green card stock; score and fold in half. Attach silver charm to jump ring. Thread green sheer ribbon through top of pale green card stock; slide jump ring onto ribbon and tie into a bow. Trim ends.

Cut a piece of pink card stock slightly smaller than front of pale green card stock; glue to pale green card stock. Layer two paper flowers and pink button; use a sewing needle to attach flowers and button together with green floss. Glue to front of pale green card stock. Glue "precious" definition across bottom of pale green card stock; glue "enduring" definition inside. Stamp an "&" inside above definition.

Cut a ½ x 5½-inch strip from pale green card stock. With long side laying parallel on work surface, score a line ½ inch from right edge; score additional lines 1½, 3 and 4 inches from right edge. Fold on scored lines forming a rectangular shape. Adhere rectangle together; adhere one of the long sides inside pale green card stock, forming a pop-up. Attach pressed daisy sticker to remaining long side.

Transfer "Mom" and "thanks" underneath sticker. Use a computer or hand print "for always being there" onto cream card stock; trim a rectangle around words and adhere inside strip. Glue assembled piece to paper, overlapping printed ribbon. Use mini brad to attach photo anchor directly underneath strip to keep strip closed. Glue assembled piece to card.

To embellish envelope, cut a strip of striped paper; adhere across bottom of envelope. Transfer pink daisy overlapping strip or stamp "Happy Mother's Day" above strip with pale green ink. ■

SOURCES: Striped paper from KI Memories; rubber stamps from Duncan; paper blossoms, photo anchor, definitions, alphabet rub-on transfers and jump ring from Making Memories; printed ribbon from Creative Impressions; pressed petal pebble sticker from Pressed Petals.

Chocolate Indulgence

Design by KATHLEEN PANEITZ

MATERIALS

Pink harlequin print paper

Light brown card stock

Envelope template to fit a
6 x 5-inch card

"celebrate" definition

Vintage chocolate label

Alphabet stamps

Assorted black alphabet
rub-on transfers

Pink metal alphabet
charms

Brown ink pad

Glue stick

Paper adhesive

Cut a 12 x 5-inch piece of light brown card stock; score and fold in half. Trim a 4½-inch-wide strip of pink harlequin print paper; adhere across center of card and trim edges. Glue vintage chocolate label across center of strip.

Stamp "INDULGE" above chocolate label. Use paper adhesive to attach pink metal alphabet charms below label in lower left corner. Transfer "deserve it!" beside alphabet charms; transfer "yourself today" on top of "INDULGE."

Use envelope template to trace and cut an envelope from light brown card stock; score and fold lines. Glue side and bottom flaps together. Trim a 3¼-inch-wide strip of harlequin print paper; apply brown ink to edges and glue across center of envelope. Trim edges.

Apply ink to edges of "celebrate" definition and glue to left edge of envelope. Transfer "Mom" above definition; transfer "on your day!" below definition. ∎

SOURCES: Printed paper from Rusty Pickle; label from Heart & Home Inc.; rubber stamps from Wordsworth; alphabet charms from Westrim Crafts; rub-on transfers from Doodlebug Design Inc.; definition and rub-on transfers from Making Memories; envelope template from The C-Thru Ruler Co.

Monogrammed Note Cards

DIAGRAM ON PAGE 150

Design by MELANIE BAUER

Cut a 5½ x 8-inch piece of white card stock; score and fold in half. Cut a 4 x 5½-inch piece of patterned paper; apply brown ink to the edges of a 3¼ x 3½-inch piece of a different patterned paper and adhere in bottom right corner. Wrap ribbon around papers and tie a knot on left side; trim ends.

Cut a 2½-inch square from gray-blue card stock; referring to photo, machine-sew ⅜ inch from each edge. Stamp initial in center of card stock; glue on top of ribbon. Glue assembled piece onto card front. Repeat for desired number of note cards varying patterned papers used.

Enlarge envelope pattern 135 percent; trace and cut an envelope from patterned paper. Score and fold on dashed lines; secure bottom and sides with glue stick. ∎

SOURCES: Patterned papers from Chatterbox; initial rubber stamp from Ma Vinci's Reliquary.

MATERIALS

Coordinating patterned papers
Gray-blue and white card stock
Large initial rubber stamp
Brown ink pad
½-inch-wide brown satin ribbon
Sewing machine with all-purpose white thread
Glue stick

Wedding Bouquet

Design by MARY AYRES

MATERIALS

Card stock: white, pale
   pink and pink
Pink envelope to fit a
   5 x 7-inch card
8 wallet-size color copies
   of rose photo
5 silver round brads
Small and medium
   metal-edge vellum
   rectangle tags
Wedding sentiment
   rub-on transfers
Pink ink pad
¹⁄₁₆-inch circle punch
Sewing machine with silver
   all-purpose thread
Instant-dry paper adhesive

Cut a 10 x 7-inch piece of pale pink card stock; score and fold in half. Adhere a 3½-inch pink square to the center of a 4½-inch white square; glue to top of card. Machine-sew a straight stitch around edges of both squares.

Determine what portion of rose photo will be featured for the folding design; cut a 1½-inch square from that same portion of each color copy. Fold each square in half diagonally with right side of photo face up; score line. Referring to photo for design, unfold squares and fold sides to scored center line, forming a point at bottom.

Ink edges of each folded photo. Determine and mark center of pink square on card. Arrange and adhere folded photos symmetrically around center dot. Punch a ¹⁄₁₆-inch hole in center of folded design; attach brad.

Transfer wedding sentiment onto medium vellum tag; position tag below folded design. Punch ¹⁄₁₆-inch holes on sides of tag; attach brads.

To embellish envelope, transfer wedding sentiment onto small vellum tag; position on envelope flap. Punch ¹⁄₁₆-inch hole on sides of tag; attach brads. ∎

SOURCES: Rub-on transfers from Royal & Langnickel; Zip Dry paper adhesive from Beacon.

Wedding Words

Design by KATHLEEN PANIETZ

Cut a 9¼ x 5⅝-inch piece of cream card stock; score and fold in half. Use a computer or hand print "Wishing you happily ever after" onto gray card stock; trim a 3½ x 5-inch rectangle around sentiment, with sentiment at bottom edge of rectangle. Ink edges with watermark ink; emboss with white embossing powder. Glue on left side of card.

Stamp love definition onto white card stock with black ink; trim a 3⅝ x 4⅛-inch rectangle around definition. Ink edges with watermark ink; emboss with silver embossing powder. Tie cream ribbon across stamped card stock. Tie a knot and trim ends into V-notches. Adhere to card.

Paint metal quote; quickly wipe excess off with paper towels, leaving paint in grooves. Let dry and glue to card.

Use envelope template to trace and cut an envelope from cream card stock; score and fold lines. Glue side and bottom flaps together. ***Note:*** *Template measurements may need to be adjusted slightly to fit card.* Stamp wedding bells onto front of envelope with black ink. ∎

SOURCES: Wedding bells rubber stamp from Stampabilities; love definition rubber stamp from Stampin' Up!; envelope template from The C-Thru Ruler Co.; metal quote from Making Memories; watermark ink pad from Tsukineko Inc.

MATERIALS

Card stock: cream, white and gray
Love definition and wedding bells rubber stamps
Envelope template to fit a 4⅝ x 5⅝-inch card
Black and watermark ink pads
White acrylic paint
White and silver embossing powders
Metal "love" quote
⅞-inch-wide cream ribbon
Embossing heat gun
Paintbrush
Paper towels
Paper adhesive
Computer font (optional)

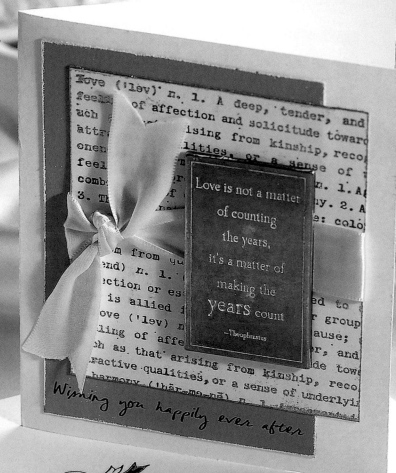

Cherish the Moment

Design by L I N D A B E E S O N

MATERIALS

Card stock: black, beige
  and moss green
Coordinating green and
  red patterned papers
Small strip script-print paper
6-inch square beige
  envelope with eyelet
  fasteners
Rub-on transfers: "Cherish
  the moment" and
  "happily ever after"
Date rub-on transfers
Silver heart charm
⅝-inch-wide red ribbon
Brown ink pad
Glue stick
Adhesive dots

Cut a 5½ x 11-inch piece of black card stock; score and fold in half. Cut a 4⅞-inch square from red patterned paper; mat onto moss green card stock. Mat again onto beige card stock.

Cut a strip from green patterned paper, varying the width. Glue across layered squares; wrap ends to reverse side and glue. Wrap small strip of script-print paper along bottom of green patterned strip; wrap and glue ends to reverse side.

Punch two ⅛-inch holes beside each other in lower left corner of green patterned strip; thread ribbon through holes. Thread heart charm onto ribbon and tie a knot; trim ends diagonally. Glue assembled piece to card.

Transfer "Cherish the moment" onto green patterned strip. Transfer desired date in lower right corner.

For envelope, thread ribbon through eyelets and tie a bow. Transfer "happily ever after" on envelope flap. ∎

SOURCES: Green and red patterned papers from Basic Grey; script-print paper from Penny Black Inc.; rub-on transfers from The C-Thru Ruler Co./Déjà Views, Making Memories and Chatterbox.

Keepsake Card

Design by STACEY STAMITOLES

Use a computer to generate, or hand-print, "Forever and Always" on gray card stock; cut a 4¼ x 1-inch rectangle around words. Center and glue rectangle to folded down portion on front of pocket card.

Cut a 4¼ x ⅞-inch rectangle from pink paisley print paper; glue to pocket card below folded portion. Punch a ⅟₁₆-inch hole through flower center; insert brad. Use an adhesive dot to attach flower to right side of pink rectangle on pocket.

Cut a 3¾ x 2⅟₁₆-inch rectangle from mint green paisley print paper; glue to bottom of tag, lining up bottom edges. Use a computer to generate, or hand-print, desired last name on pink paisley print paper. Cut a 3¾ x 1½-inch rectangle around name; glue to tag ⅟₁₆-inch above top edge of mint green rectangle.

Use a computer to generate, or hand-print, "Mr. & Mrs." on mint green paisley print paper; cut a 3¾ x 1½-inch rectangle around words. Glue to top portion of tag ⅟₁₆-inch above top edge of pink rectangle. Trim edges of papers even with tag.

Punch a ⅛-inch hole at top of tag. Cut a 6-inch length of ribbon; fold in half and thread through hole in tag. Thread ribbon ends through formed loop; pull to secure. Insert tag inside pocket. ∎

SOURCES: Printed papers from Anna Griffin Inc.; card set and flower from Making Memories.

MATERIALS

Ivory tag and pocket
   card set
Card stock: gray
Printed papers: mint green
   paisley, pink paisley
¹¹⁄₁₆-inch-wide green
   satin ribbon
Paper flower
Pink mini round brad
⅟₁₆- and ⅛-inch
   hole punches
Adhesive dots
Glue stick
Computer font (optional)

Two Lives

Design by KATHLEEN PANIETZ

MATERIALS

Yellow word print paper
Cream textured paper
White card stock
Envelope template to fit a
    5½-inch square card
Gold wedding quote
    stickers
Cream paper flowers
White mini brads
⅞-inch-wide sheer
    white ribbon
Glue stick

Cut a 5½ x 11-inch piece of white card stock; score and fold in half. Cover front of card with yellow word print paper; trim edges even with card.

Attach desired wedding quote onto cream textured paper; trim a rectangle around sentiment. Layer onto white card stock; trim a small border. Center and glue to card.

Attach three paper flowers around sentiment by inserting mini brads through flower centers. Tie a bow with sheer ribbon; trim ends and glue along left side of sentiment.

Use envelope template to trace and cut an envelope from white card stock; score and fold lines. Glue side and bottom flaps together. Cover envelope flap with yellow print paper; trim edges even. Attach desired stickers to front of envelope. ■

SOURCES: Patterned paper and stickers from Creative Imaginations; textured paper from Lasting Impressions for Paper Inc.; paper flowers from Making Memories; envelope from The C-Thru Ruler Co.

Beautiful Things

Design by J E A N K I E V L A N

Cut and adhere a piece of green card stock to front of card; cut metallic gold paper ⅛-inch smaller on all sides than green card stock. Adhere gold paper to card.

Cut a rectangle from section of tulip print paper that includes a butterfly; trim rectangle ⅛-inch smaller on all sides than gold paper. Cut tulip and butterfly images from embossed vellum; glue images to their corresponding images on paper. Use craft knife to cut around edge of butterfly's right wing. Bend wing upward slightly.

Layer vellum sentiment onto gold textured paper; trim edges, leaving a small border. Layer again onto green card stock; trim edges, leaving a small border.

Glue tulip paper rectangle to front of card, being careful not to glue down butterfly's ring wing. Referring to photo, glue layered sentiment underneath butterfly's right wing.

To embellish envelope, trace envelope flap onto the reverse side of tulip print paper. Cut piece out and adhere to flap. Cut a ¼-inch-wide strip of gold textured paper; glue along bottom of envelope flap. Trim edges even. Trim a butterfly image from embossed vellum and adhere onto flap. ■

SOURCES: Permanent adhesive cartridges and applicator from Xyron; red tulip paper and vellum from K&Company; vellum quote from Die Cuts With A View.

MATERIALS

Ivory greeting card
   with envelope
12 x 12-inch sheet red
   tulip print paper
12 x 12-inch sheet
   embossed tulip
   print vellum
8½ x 11-inch metallic gold
   textured paper
8½ x 11-inch green
   card stock
Desired sentiment printed
   on vellum
Craft knife
Permanent adhesive
   cartridges with
   applicator

The best and most beautiful things in the world cannot be seen or even touched... They must be felt with the heart.

Flower Bubble

Design by MEREDITH HOLMAN

MATERIALS

4¼ x 5½-inch ivory flecked card with envelope

Card stock: orange, blue and white

Patterned papers: striped, polka-dot and floral

³⁄₁₆-inch-wide green gingham ribbon

Clear flower bubble sticker

Flower punch

Small hole punch

Glue stick

Cut a 4 x 5¼-inch piece of orange card stock; tear right vertical edge. Cut a ½ x 5¼-inch strip of striped paper. Referring to photo, glue striped paper toward right edge of card; glue torn orange card stock overlapping striped paper. Line up top and bottom edges.

Tear a piece of blue card stock and a piece of striped paper; overlap and glue to card. Layer a 2-inch polka-dot square onto a 2⅛-inch white card stock square. Wrap green gingham ribbon around square and tie two knots. Trim ends. Attach flower bubble sticker to square and glue to card.

To embellish envelope, cover envelope flap with orange card stock. Trim edges even. Cut a 1½-inch-wide strip of floral print paper; tear top horizontal edge and glue to envelope flap. Trim edges even.

Cut a 1¼-inch square from polka-dot paper; layer onto white and orange card stock, trimming edges. Punch a flower from orange card stock and a small circle from white card stock. Glue circle to flower; glue flower to square. Glue square to envelope flap. ■

SOURCES: Patterned papers from Chatterbox; sticker from Pebbles Inc.

Merci

Design by STACEY STAMITOLES

Apply black ink to edges of slotted card; referring to photo, transfer "merci" onto card. Trim patterned paper to 8½ x 3¼ inches; apply black ink to edges and slide paper into card. Attach flower at top of card with adhesive dots. Tie two pieces of ribbon around card and tie into knots. Trim ends.

Using burgundy acrylic paint, stamp decorative accents in bottom corners on envelope and onto envelope flap. Let dry. Punch a 1½-inch circle from patterned paper; adhere onto metal-edge tag. Transfer "thank you" onto tag. Attach tag to envelope with adhesive dots. Cut a piece of patterned paper to fit opposite end of envelope; ink edges and adhere. Cut a ¼-inch-wide strip of a different patterned paper and attach along left side of piece. Punch two decorative corners from patterned paper; position in a square shape in upper corner of envelope and adhere. ■

SOURCES: Slotted card, envelope, rub-on transfer and foam stamps from Making Memories; patterned paper from Basic Grey; corner punch from EK Success.

MATERIALS

Olive green slotted card with envelope
Coordinating patterned papers
"Merci" and "thank you" rub-on transfers
Burgundy acrylic paint
Black ink pad
Metal-edge circle tag
Decorative accent foam stamp
Yellow silk flower
¼-inch-wide yellow/burgundy ribbon
Corner punch
1½-inch circle punch
Adhesive dots
Double-sided tape

MATERIALS

4¼ x 6-inch black card
   with envelope
Brightly colored
   striped paper
Lime green card stock
Shrink plastic
Black string
Flower rubber stamp
Colored pencils
Black ink pad
Small hole punch
Tweezers
Heat embossing gun
Sandpaper
Adhesive dots
Glue stick

Floral Fiesta

Design by S T A C E Y   S T A M I T O L E S

Lightly sand shrink plastic and stamp flower; let ink dry. Color stamped image with colored pencils. Punch a small hole at top of image. Use tweezers to hold image down onto a heat resistant surface; heat with embossing gun until plastic curls and shrinks. Press down on plastic with a flat, heat resistant item to flatten plastic while it is still hot. Tie string through hole; trim string ends and set aside. Repeat process to make an additional plastic flower.

Glue a 3¼ x 6-inch piece of striped paper down center of card. Cut a 1⅝ x 3¼-inch piece of lime green card stock; tear bottom edge. Ink edges. Center and glue to card. Use an adhesive dot to attach stamped flower to card.

To embellish envelope, glue a 3⅜-inch-wide strip of striped paper across envelope. Trim ends even. Cut a 1⅝ x 2¾-inch rectangle from lime green card stock; tear bottom edge. Ink edges and glue in upper left corner of envelope. Attach remaining stamped flower to lime green rectangle with an adhesive dot.

Glue a 1-inch-wide strip of striped paper along bottom edge of envelope flap; trim edges even with flap. ∎

SOURCES: Patterned paper from Mara Mi Inc.; card and envelope from Hero Arts; rubber stamp from Endless Creations Inc.

Friendship Greetings DIAGRAM ON PAGE 150

Design by JENNIFER HANSEN

Cut a 7⅜ x 10⅞-inch piece of double-sided card stock; score and fold in half with striped paper on the outside. Center and glue a 7⅜ x ⅝-inch strip of dark purple card stock onto a 7⅜ x 1½-inch strip of double-sided card stock, with purple side face up. Glue strips to a 7⅜ x 2⅝-inch strip of floral print vellum. Center and glue to card horizontally, applying glue only in places where it will not be seen through the vellum.

Stamp flower image onto slide mount; emboss with light purple embossing powder. ***Note:*** *Remove heat immediately if edges of slide mount start to curl.* Adhere to card diagonally on left side of layered strips. Glue alphabet charms along strip to spell "FRIEND."

Referring to diagram, cut out an envelope from double-sided card stock with purple side on the outside. Score and fold dashed lines; glue side and bottom flaps together.

Layer a 1⅛-inch-wide strip of floral print vellum onto a 2-inch-wide strip of double-sided card stock, with the striped side face up. Layer onto white card stock, trimming edges. Glue along left edge of envelope; trim edges even. ∎

SOURCES: Double-sided card stock and floral print vellum from American Crafts; alphabet charms from Junkitz; watermark ink pad from Tsukineko Inc.; rubber stamp and embossing powder from Stampin' Up!.

MATERIALS

Card stock: double-sided striped/purple, dark purple and white
Floral print vellum
Purple solid slide mount
Alphabet circle charms
Flower stamp
Light purple embossing powder
Watermark ink pad
Embossing heat gun
Paper adhesive

Things I Love About Summer

Design by MARY AYRES

MATERIALS

Card stock: white, pink, yellow and 7 shades of blue and turquoise

2 (1¼-inch) and 7 (¾-inch) wooden circles

Silver heart brad

Square alphabet rub-on transfers

Summer-themed word label stickers

Summer-themed word metal strips

Dimensional number stickers

White business-size envelope

Yellow and blue ink pads

Ultrafine iridescent glitter

Decorative-edge scissors

1⁄16-inch hole punch

Craft sponge

Gem adhesive

Paper adhesive

Cut a 7½ x 9-inch rectangle from white card stock; score and fold in half. To form "waves" on front of card, cut seven 5 x 1¼-inch strips from turquoise and blue card stock. Trim the top edge of each strip with decorative-edge scissors; use craft sponge to rub blue ink along decorative edges. Referring to photo and beginning approximately 2½ inches from top of card, layer and adhere strips across card. Trim edges evenly along edges of card.

Ink all wooden circles with yellow ink. Use paper adhesive to glue ¾-inch wooden circles on the left end of each "wave" strip. Use gem adhesive to apply a small amount of iridescent glitter to a few number stickers; let dry and attach number stickers, in numerical order, to wooden circles on card. Randomly adhere summer-themed word label stickers and metal strips beside each circle.

Cut a 3¾ x 1-inch strip from pink card stock; ink edges with blue ink. Glue strip above blue and turquoise strips. Transfer "summer" onto pink strip.

To form sun, use decorative-edge scissors to cut a 1½-inch-diameter circle from yellow card stock; ink edges with blue ink. With craft sponge, dab a small amount of gem adhesive on edges of circle and apply iridescent glitter. Glue a large wooden circle to yellow circle. Transfer "joy" onto wooden circle and glue in upper left corner of card.

Adhere "Things I" and "About" word strips in upper right corner of card; punch a 1⁄16-inch hole between word strips and attach heart brad.

To embellish envelope, cut a ¾ x 4-inch strip from pink card stock. Ink edges with blue ink and glue along left side of envelope. Following instructions above, make another sun, transferring "Share the Joy" onto wooden circle instead of "joy." Glue circle to top of pink strip. ∎

SOURCES: Rub-on transfers, metal word strips, number and word stickers from K&Company; wooden circles from Forster; Gem-Tac adhesive from Beacon.

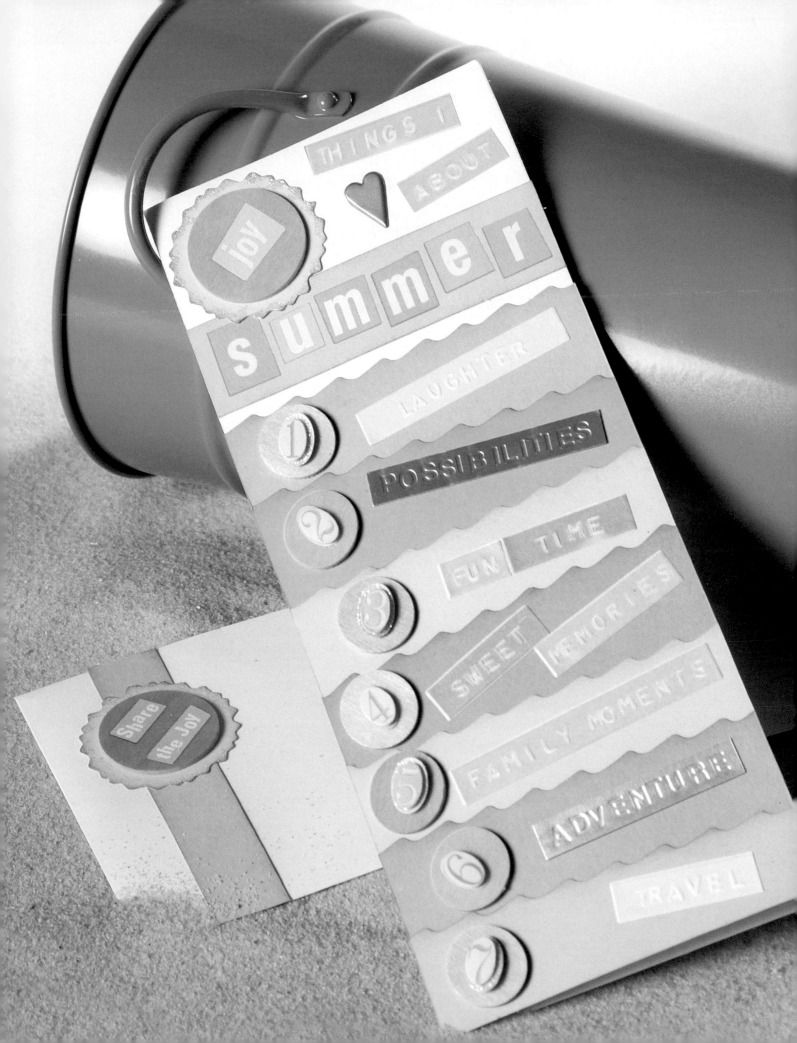

MATERIALS

Card stock: brown, cream
    and off-white
Black and white floral
    print paper
Rubber stamps: fork, knife,
    spoon, handwriting
    background, "you're
    invited" and alphabet
Ink pads: black solvent-
    based, black and brown
Brown envelope to fit a
    5½ x 4¼-inch card
Metallic silver square
    bookplate
Brown eyelets with eyelet
    setting tool
Brown and black fibers
Sandpaper
Sewing machine with black
    all-purpose thread
Paper adhesive

Summer Picnic Invite

Design by LINDA BEESON

Use black ink to stamp the knife, fork and spoon images onto off-white card stock; trim a ¾ x 2⅜-inch rectangle around each piece of flatware. Use brown ink to stamp handwriting background onto a 3-inch square of cream card stock. Rub brown ink on edges of rectangles and square. Machine-stitch flatware rectangles across handwriting square, evenly spaced.

Cut a 5½ x 8½-inch piece of brown card stock; score and fold in half. Tear an approximately 4⅛ x 3¾-inch rectangle from black and white floral print paper. Position rectangle on left side of card at a slight angle; machine-stitch rectangle to card. Glue flatware square on right side of card, at a slight angle, overlapping torn rectangle.

Sand silver bookplate; rub black solvent-based ink over bookplate. Sand bookplate again. Stamp "Please Come" onto cream card stock with black ink; trim a square around sentiment to fit onto bookplate. Rub brown ink on square; glue on reverse side of bookplate. Tie fibers onto each end of bookplate and adhere to card, referring to photo for placement.

Attach eyelets in lower corners on front of card; thread fibers through eyelets. Tie fibers into a knot and trim ends, if needed.

To embellish envelope, use black ink to stamp "you're invited" onto off-white card stock; trim a rectangle around sentiment and rub brown ink on edges. Use brown ink to stamp handwriting background onto off-white card stock. Center and glue "you're invited" rectangle on top of handwriting background; trim a ⅜-inch border. Rub brown ink on edges. Glue layered rectangle in lower right corner on front of envelope. ■

SOURCES: Rubber stamps from 100 Proof Press Inc., Penny Black Inc., Savvy Stamps and Duncan; solvent-based ink pad from Tsukineko Inc.; patterned paper from Chatterbox Inc.; bookplate from Die Cuts With A View.

Happy Day
DIAGRAM ON PAGE 152

Design by J U L I E   E B E R S O L E

Cut a 4¼ x 8½-inch piece of light sage green card stock; score and fold in half, forming a 4¼-inch square card. With card open and referring to Cutting Diagram on page 152, use a craft knife to cut along the dashed lines as indicated on card front. Fold the sides back, revealing a 1¾ x 1⅝-inch window. Punch a ¹⁄₁₆-inch hole through the center of each folded side; insert brads.

Using brown ink, stamp tree inside card, positioning it to show through window; use pale blue chalk ink to stamp scallop-edge oval to the upper right area of tree. Color tree with markers. Punch a ³⁄₁₆-inch hole through tire hanging from tree image; set black eyelet.

Thread ribbon through card; knot ends together on front and trim. Use black ink to stamp "happy day!" in lower right corner on card front.

For envelope, choose which side of printed paper will be front of envelope; lay printed paper front side down on work surface. Use pattern provided on page 152 to trace and cut an envelope from printed paper. Score and fold along dashed lines to form envelope flaps, but do not glue them together yet. Mark positions on top envelope flap and directly below it for eyelet fasteners. Open envelope up.

Cut a 7-inch length of twine. Punch two ½-inch circles from kraft card stock; place one circle on marked position on top envelope flap; punch a ¹⁄₁₆-inch hole through center of circle. Insert one end of twine through punched hole and set a sage green eyelet, securing circle and twine. Repeat for remaining circle, attaching it directly below envelope flap. Do not attach twine to second circle.

Refold envelope; glue side and bottom flaps together. Round corners of top envelope flap with corner punch. To close, wrap twine around eyelet fasteners. ■

SOURCES: Printed paper from Chatterbox Inc.; rubber stamps from A Muse Artstamps; chalk ink pad from Clearsnap Inc.

MATERIALS

Card stock: light sage green, kraft

Printed paper: light brown floral

Rubber stamps: tree with tire swing, scallop-edge oval, "happy day!"

Ink pads: pale blue chalk, black pigment, brown pigment

Markers

³⁄₁₆-inch-wide black gingham ribbon

Twine

2 black mini round brads

Round eyelets: 1 black, 2 sage green

Eyelet setting tool

Punches: rounded corner, ½-inch circle, ¹⁄₁₆-inch circle, ³⁄₁₆-inch circle

Craft knife

Glue stick

MATERIALS

Blue and yellow card stock

Coordinating striped
    paper

Blue 7-inch-long zipper

"Summer" label tag

Mini safety pin

Summer-themed words
    rub-on transfers

Stapler with blue staples

Envelope template to fit
    a 5 x 7-inch card

Glue stick

Permanent paper adhesive

Soak Up the Sun

Design by TAMI MAYBERRY

Cut a 10 x 7-inch piece of blue card stock; score and fold in half. Cut a 5 x 7-inch piece of striped paper. Mark a point 4¾ inches down left edge; mark another point on top edge 3 inches from left side. Line up points with a ruler; draw a light pencil line. Cut along pencil line to cut off upper left portion. Adhere to front of card.

Unzip zipper approximately halfway down; position zipper along left edge of card, laying right side of zipper along diagonal edge of striped paper. Use paper adhesive to attach zipper to card.

Staple "Summer" tag to top left edge of card. Transfer "relax" to blue card stock; trim a rectangle around word. Attach mini safety pin in upper left corner of rectangle; attach safety pin through zipper pull.

Transfer "soak up the sun" and "kick back" onto blue card stock; trim rectangles around each sentiment and glue rectangles in lower right corner of card.

Use envelope template to trace and cut an envelope from yellow card stock; score and fold envelope flaps. Glue side and bottom flaps together. ∎

SOURCES: Striped paper from Chatterbox Inc.; tag from Junkitz; blue staples from Making Memories; rub-on transfers from Royal & Langnickel; Coluzzle envelope template from Provo Craft.

Sunflower Defined

Design by KATHLEEN PANEITZ

Cut a 9 x 5⅞-inch piece of orange card stock; score and fold in half. With stripes horizontal, center and glue a 4¼ x 5½-inch piece of striped paper to card front.

Drag light brown ink pad across an entire sheet of cream card stock. Use a computer to generate, or hand-print, "sunflower" in different sizes on inked card stock. Cut a 3¾ x 3¹⁄₁₆-inch rectangle around words; ink edges with brown ink. Glue to top portion of card.

Use a computer to generate, or hand-print, sunflower definition on another sheet of inked card stock. Trim a rectangle around definition; ink edges with brown ink. Glue to lower left corner of card. Attach quilled sticker to lower right corner of card.

For envelope, use template to trace and cut an envelope from striped paper with stripes horizontal. Score and fold envelope flaps; glue side and bottom flaps together.

Using watermark ink, stamp the top flower portion of sunflower to lower left corner on front of envelope. Sprinkle with copper embossing powder; emboss. ∎

SOURCES: Printed paper from Scenic Route Paper Co.; sticker from EK Success; foam stamp from Duncan; ink pads from Ranger and Tsukineko Inc.; template from The C-Thru Ruler Co.

MATERIALS

Card stock: orange, cream
Printed paper: golden
    yellow striped
Quilled sunflower sticker
Sunflower definition
Sunflower foam stamp
Ink pads: watermark, light
    brown antique-finish,
    brown dye
Copper embossing
    powder
Embossing heat tool
Envelope template to fit a
    4½ x 5⅞-inch card
Glue stick
Computer font (optional)

MATERIALS

5 x 7-inch script-writing
    patterned tag-shaped
    card with envelope
Light tan and black
    card stock
Paris map paper
Clear vellum
$\frac{9}{16}$-inch-wide tan ribbon
2 round travel clasps
    with string
2 gold suspender clips
4 gold mini round brads
"Dear FATHER" gold
    rub-on transfer
2½ x 3¼-inch father-
    themed photo
Sewing machine with black
    all-purpose thread
$\frac{1}{16}$-inch hole punch
Black adhesive foam squares
Paper adhesive
Computer font (optional)

Dear Father

Design by MARY AYRES

Cut a rectangle from map paper ¼ inch larger on all sides than photo. Machine-stitch ⅛ inch from edges of rectangle; machine-stitch ⅛ inch from edges on front of card. Glue photo to rectangle and glue rectangle angled toward bottom of card.

Cut a 6 x 1¾-inch rectangle from light tan card stock; transfer "Dear FATHER" angled across center of strip. Cut a 6 x 2-inch rectangle from black card stock; glue light tan rectangle to black rectangle. Place strip angled across top portion of card; trim ends evenly with card. Remove strip from card and machine-stitch ⅛ inch from edges on light tan strip. Use adhesive foam squares to attach strip to card.

Use a computer font or hand-print "You are the Best" onto vellum; tear a rectangle around words. Place vellum strip angled across bottom of photo. Punch a ¹⁄₁₆-inch hole at each end of strip; attach brads.

Referring to photo, adhere round travel clasps to the left and right of photo; wrap string around clasps several times and tie into a knot in center. Trim ends of string. Attach suspender clips to top of light tan and black strip; thread ribbon through holes at top of card and through suspender clips. Tie a bow and trim ends into V-notches.

To embellish envelope, use computer font or hand-print "Happy Father's Day" onto light tan card stock. Trim a ¾-inch-wide strip around sentiment and layer onto black card stock. Trim a small border along top and bottom edges. Glue strip angled across envelope flap; trim ends evenly with flap. Punch a ¹⁄₁₆-inch hole at each end of strip; attach brads. ∎

SOURCES: Card, patterned paper, ribbon and string clasp from K&Company; rub-on transfer from Royal & Langnickel.

Dear *FATHER*

You are the Best

Happy Father's

Daddy's Pocket

Design by TAMI MAYBERRY

MATERIALS

Light blue and blue
    card stock

Blue block patterned paper

"Dad" label tag

Light blue mini safety pin

Small black and white photo

Die-cutting tool with
    pocket die

Black and light blue ink pads

Black pen

Envelope template to fit
    a 5 x 7-inch card

Glue stick

Computer font (optional)

Score and fold a 10 x 7-inch piece of light blue card stock in half, forming a 5 x 7-inch card. Rub light blue ink on card edges. Center and adhere a 4½ x 6½-inch piece of patterned paper to card front.

Use pocket die and die-cutting tool to cut a pocket from blue card stock. Use a computer font or hand-print the following sentiment onto pocket: "A Daddy is a man who has photos in his wallet where his money used to be." Rub black ink along edges of pocket; trace stitch lines with black pen.

Adhere pocket to card, leaving top edge unattached. Attach mini safety pin at top of "Dad" tag. Position photo and tag inside pocket and adhere to secure.

For envelope, use envelope template to trace and cut an envelope from blue patterned paper. Score and fold envelope flaps; glue side and bottom flaps together. ■

SOURCES: Patterned paper from Provo Craft; die and die-cutting tool from Sizzix/Ellison; tag from Junkitz; safety pin from Making Memories; Coluzzle envelope template from Provo Craft.

Tools for Dad

Design by SUSAN HUBER

Cut a 5½ x 8½-inch piece of tan card stock; score and fold in half. Rub brown ink on edges. Center and glue a 5¼ x 4-inch piece of dark blue textured paper to card.

Cut a 5¼ x 1⅝-inch strip of cork. Stamp various tools across cork strip. Punch a ¹⁄₁₆-inch hole in each corner of cork; attach copper brads.

Cut approximately a 3-foot-long piece of wire; run wire through paper crimper to create a zigzag effect. Wrap zigzagged wire around cork strip, crisscrossing pieces on front. Attach cork strip to bottom portion of card, securing wire ends underneath.

Die-cut three hammers and three screwdrivers from dark blue textured paper and silver paper. Piece die cuts together so top portion of tools are silver and the bottom portions are dark blue. Attach tools across cork strip with small pieces of adhesive foam tape.

Cut three 1⅛-inch squares from cork. Attach alphabet stickers to squares, spelling "DAD." Punch a ¹⁄₁₆-inch hole on left and right sides of squares; insert light blue and dark blue brads. Attach cork squares at top of card.

Use envelope template to trace and cut an envelope from tan textured card stock; score and fold envelope flaps. Glue side and bottom flaps together.

Stamp large saw image on envelope flap; center and stamp image again on front of envelope. Stamp tool images along top and bottom edges on envelope front. ◼

SOURCES: Textured paper from Emagination Crafts; stickers from Cloud 9 Design; dies and die-cutting tool from QuicKutz; rubber stamps from Darcie's Country Folk; wire from Artistic Wire; Coluzzle envelope template from Provo Craft.

MATERIALS

Tan and tan textured card stock
Dark blue textured paper
Silver metallic paper
Cork sheet
Blue alphabet square stickers
Mini round brads: copper, light blue and dark blue
Mini hammer and screwdriver dies with die-cutting tool
Rubber stamps: screwdriver, pliers, wrench and large saw
Brown ink pad
Thin silver wire
Envelope template to fit a 5½ x 4¼-inch card
¹⁄₁₆-inch hole punch
Paper crimper
Wire nippers
Glue stick
Double-sided adhesive sheets
Adhesive foam tape

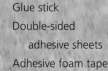

All Hail the Chief

Design by BARBARA GREVE

MATERIALS

Blue distressed patterned
   paper
Coordinating square
   patterned paper
White paper
2 coordinating tags
Square acrylic alphabet
   charms
Blue acrylic tie button
Blue, orange and black
   alphabet rub-on
   transfers
Bottle cap
Hemp cord: light blue,
   dark blue and yellow
Dark blue embroidery
   thread
¾-inch gold pin back
1-inch circle punch
Sewing needle
⅛-inch anywhere punch
   with hammer
Paintbrushes
Paper towels
Satin-finish decoupage
   medium
Matte-finish varnish
Blue acrylic paint
Gel stain medium
High-gloss polymer
   compound
Acid-free permanent glue
Clear dimensional
   silicone glue
Computer font (optional)

Cut blue distressed paper 11 x 7 inches; score and fold in half, forming a 5½ x 7-inch card. Cut a 4¾ x 6½-inch rectangle from coordinating patterned paper. Set aside.

Use a computer font or hand-print "Chief" onto white paper; punch a 1-inch circle around word. Attach word inside bottle cap with decoupage medium. Allow to dry and apply a coat of varnish over word. Let dry.

Mix equal amounts of blue paint and gel stain medium; stain decoupaged word with mixture. Wipe excess stain off with paper towels until desired effect is achieved. Allow to dry.

Following manufacturer's instructions, pour the high-gloss polymer compound into bottle cap. Pour to desired thickness, but do not exceed ⅛ inch. Allow to dry overnight.

Punch two ⅛-inch holes on right side of tag with side handles; position tag on center of patterned paper rectangle and mark placement of holes. Use anywhere punch to punch holes through paper. Referring to photo, thread dark and light blue cord through holes and tie on both tags. Tie a knot and trim cord; unravel ends to form fringe. Using different color alphabet rub-ons, transfer "all hail" on first tag and "the" at the top of front tag, leaving room for bottle cap.

Thread yellow hemp cord through the handles of the first tag, wrapping cord ends around to reverse side of paper. Use acid-free glue to adhere assembled piece to card, securing cord ends underneath.

Attach "dad" alphabet squares above tags with silicone glue. Use same glue to attach pin back to bottle cap. Thread sewing needle with blue embroidery thread; sew tie button onto card beside alphabet squares.

Position bottle cap pin on front tag; make marks at each side of pin. Punch holes at marks. Attach pin to tag through holes. ■

SOURCES: Patterned papers and tags from Basic Grey; alphabet squares from Doodlebug Design Inc.; rub-on transfers from Scrapworks Inc., Making Memories and Doodlebug Design Inc.; tie button from Junkitz; gel stain medium, decoupage medium, varnish and acid-free permanent glue from Delta; high-gloss polymer compound from Environmental Technology Inc.

Dad's Gone Fishing

Design by DEANNA HUTCHISON

Cut a 5⅝ x 8¼-inch piece of dark olive green card stock; score and fold in half. Cut a 5¼ x 3⅞-inch rectangle from light olive green patterned paper; tear in half diagonally, from corner to corner. Tear approximately ¾ inch from each torn edge to create a gap when adhered. Layer torn pieces onto a 5½ x 4-inch olive green rectangle. Rub brown ink onto entire piece.

Carefully apply brown ink to one skeleton leaf; adhere at an angle onto layered card stock with mini adhesive dots.

Use brown ink and large alphabet stamps to stamp "DAD" onto dark olive green card stock; tear a rectangle around word and rub brown ink onto rectangle. Punch a ⅛-inch hole on lower right corner of rectangle; attach brad. Glue, slightly angled, across top portion of card stock.

Rub brown ink onto hemp cord; wrap cord around left side of card stock three times, overlapping "DAD" rectangle. Secure cord ends on reverse side with tape.

Use black solvent-based ink and small alphabet stamps to stamp "Gone Fishing" onto metal sign. Hang sign from brad and secure with adhesive foam tape. Adhere assembled piece to card.

To embellish envelope, rub brown ink over entire surface, front and back. Stamp "Happy Father's Day" on left side of envelope front. Carefully apply brown ink to skeleton leaf; adhere leaf with mini adhesive dots in lower right corner on front of envelope, folding bottom edge of leaf around to reverse side of envelope. Rub brown ink onto hemp cord; thread several beads onto cord. Wrap cord around bottom of envelope three times, positioning beads as desired; tie knot on front and trim ends. Secure cord to envelope with mini adhesive dots. ■

SOURCES: Patterned paper from All My Memories; rubber stamps from FontWerks and Duncan; solvent-based ink pad from Tsukineko Inc.

MATERIALS

Dark olive green and olive green card stock
Light olive green patterned paper
Olive green envelope to fit a 5⅝ x 4⅛-inch card
Cream skeleton leaves
Brown and black solvent-based ink pads
Large and small alphabet rubber stamps
Small rustic metal sign
Hemp cord
Gold, amber and dark brown E beads
Round brad
⅛-inch hole punch
Mini adhesive dots
Adhesive foam tape
Glue stick
Tape

Crazy for Ice Cream

Design by S U S A N   S T R I N G F E L L O W

MATERIALS

Card stock: pink, white,
  pink/brown striped and
  pink/brown patterned
  double-sided
Card stock circle punch
  outs: yellow, pink
  and brown
White alphabet rub-on
  transfers
White metal spiral clip
3 white circle metal frames
3 white mini round studs
5/16-inch-wide brown sheer
  ribbon and 3/8-inch-
  wide pink polka-dot
  ribbon
Small ice cream cone and
  alphabet rubber stamps
Black ink pad
Envelope template to fit a
  6-inch square card
1½- and 1¼-inch
  circle punches
Sandpaper
Paper adhesive
Computer font (optional)

Cut a 12 x 6-inch piece of pink card stock; score and fold in half. Cut a 5½ x 5¾-inch piece of double-sided card stock. Use a computer font or hand-print "I scream, You scream, We all scream for" on bottom portion of card stock on pink patterned side. Referring to photo, score and fold the top right corner down to reveal reverse patterned side. Lightly sand edges, including corner fold.

Cut two 3-inch lengths of brown ribbon and one 3-inch length of pink polka-dot ribbon; tie each ribbon onto the spiral clip. Attach clip to folded corner. Center and adhere assembled piece to card. Secure clip with adhesive.

Use white alphabet rub-ons to transfer "ice cream!" onto pink patterned card stock to finish sentiment on front of card.

Cut a 1¼ x 6-inch strip from pink and brown striped card stock, with stripes running horizontally; sand edges of strip and glue along left edge of card. Attach a mini stud at each end of strip; attach remaining mini stud in lower right corner of card.

Stamp an ice-cream cone image onto each circle punch out; place each punch out inside a metal frame. Attach frames along edge of striped piece of card stock on card.

For envelope, use template to trace and cut an envelope from white card stock. Score and fold on envelope flaps; glue side and bottom flaps together. Cut a 5¾-inch square from double-sided card stock; lightly sand edges and glue to front of envelope with pink side face up.

Cut a 3/16 x 6-inch strip from striped card stock, with stripes running horizontally. Glue strip down left side of pink patterned card stock ⅛ inch from edge.

Punch a 1½-inch-diameter circle from white card stock. Punch a 1¼-inch-diameter circle from striped card stock; sand edges of striped circle and glue to white circle. Stamp ice-cream cone and "to" onto striped circle; glue layered circle onto front of envelope. ∎

SOURCES: Patterned card stock, circle punch outs, clip, frames, studs and rub-on transfers from Scrapworks Inc.; rubber stamp from Close To My Heart; Coluzzle envelope template from Provo Craft.

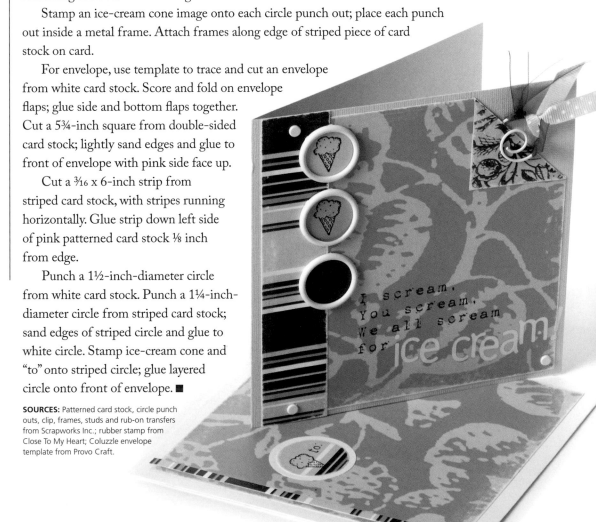

Watermelon Day

Design by TAMI MAYBERRY

Score and fold a 10 x 7-inch piece of green card stock in half, forming a 5 x 7-inch card. Use a computer to generate, or hand-print, "You're One in a Melon" on green card stock; trim a 3½ x 4-inch rectangle around words. Glue rectangle to gingham paper. Trim a small border.

Punch three ¹⁄₁₆-inch holes, evenly spaced, below words; insert brads. Ink edges. Glue assembled piece to card approximately ¼ inch from top edge.

Use die-cutting tool to cut watermelons from red and green craft foam; glue red portions to green portions to form two watermelons; color in seed shapes with black marker. Referring to photo for placement, attach left watermelon to card with adhesive dots; use foam dots to attach remaining watermelon to card, overlapping first watermelon.

For envelope, use template to trace and cut an envelope from green card stock. Score and fold envelope flaps; glue side and bottom flaps together.

Cut a 2 x 5-inch strip of gingham paper; glue along left side of envelope. Stamp "Thinking of You" on strip. ■

SOURCES: Printed paper from Rusty Pickle; die and die-cutting tool from Sizzix/Ellison; rubber stamp from River City Rubber Works; ink pad from Ranger; Coluzzle envelope template from Provo Craft.

MATERIALS

Green card stock
Printed paper: green
    gingham
Craft foam: red, green
Die-cutting tool and
    watermelon die
"Thinking of You"
    rubber stamp
Brown antique-finish
    ink pad
Black marker
3 green mini round brads
¹⁄₁₆-inch hole punch
Envelope template to fit
    a 5 x 7-inch card
Adhesive foam dots
Adhesive dots
Computer font (optional)

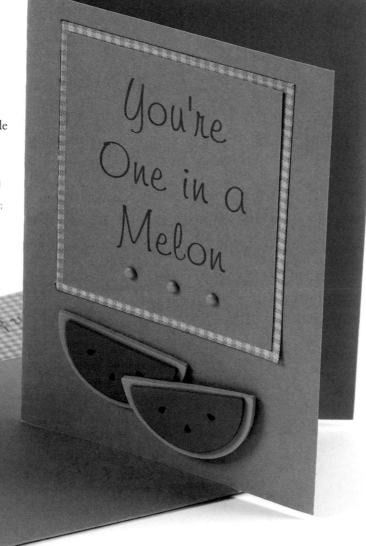

MATERIALS

3-inch square olive green
    cards with envelopes
Brightly colored acrylic
    square embellishments
Alphabet rubber stamps
Black pigment ink pad
Clear embossing powder
Acrylic paints: white,
    orange, red, blue,
    lime green
⅛-inch-wide red polka-dot
    ribbon
Orange rickrack
Highlighter marker cap
Embossing heat tool
⅛-inch hole punch
Foam brush
Adhesive dots

Little Notes

Design by GRETCHEN SCHMIDT

Using a foam brush, lightly apply white paint to center section of each card in a swiping motion. Let dry. Stamp desired sentiments at bottom of each card; sprinkle letters with clear embossing powder and emboss. Use adhesive dots to attach a square embellishment to each.

To decorate envelopes, use a highlighter marker cap and acrylic paints to stamp desired number of circles in assorted colors on envelope fronts. Let dry. If desired, punch a ⅛-inch hole through corner of envelope and thread rickrack or ribbon through hole. Tie a knot and trim ends. ■

SOURCES: Cards from Die Cuts With A View; acrylic embellishments from KI Memories; rubber stamps from K&Company.

Shells in the Sand

Design by S U S A N   H U B E R

Score and fold a 5½ x 8½-inch piece of pale purple card stock in half to form a 5½ x 4¼-inch card. Use glue stick to adhere a 5½ x 4¼-inch piece of robin's egg blue print paper to card. Round corners with corner punch. Cut a 5½ x 8½-inch piece of vellum with gold and silver flecks; score and fold in half. Round corners with corner punch

Stamp seashells and starfish onto front of folded vellum; emboss with white embossing powder. Turn vellum over and color in the reverse side of images with markers. Turn vellum back over and place on a mouse pad; use sewing needle to poke tiny holes approximately ¹⁄₁₆ inch apart around each embossed image.

Slip folded vellum over card; punch two ⅛-inch holes in upper right corner. Thread ribbon through and tie in a bow. Trim ribbon ends. Use gold thread to tie on a starfish charm. If desired, stamp another seashell image onto clear vellum; emboss and color reverse side of image. Cut out and glue seashell inside card.

Use envelope template to trace and cut an envelope from clear vellum; score and fold lines. Tape side and bottom flaps together. Stamp starfish image on envelope flap; emboss with white embossing powder. Color reverse side of starfish; pierce holes around image in same manner as above. ∎

SOURCES: Printed paper from Provo Craft; rubber stamps from Embossing Arts; watermark ink pad from Tsukineko Inc.

MATERIALS

Pale purple card stock
Robin's egg blue
    printed paper
Vellum with gold and
    silver flecks
Clear vellum
Envelope template to fit a
    5½ x 4¼-inch card
Assorted starfish and shell
    rubber stamps
Watermark ink pad
White embossing powder
Markers
¼-inch-wide blue ribbon
Starfish charm
Embossing heat tool
Rounded corner punch
⅛-inch hole punch
Mouse pad
Sewing needle
Vellum tape
Glue stick

Summer Escape

Design by KATHLEEN PANEITZ

MATERIALS

Card stock: white, blue
    textured and light brown
Vacation-themed stickers
"relax" definition
Metal feet plaque
"leave it all behind"
    rub-on transfer
Sandals in the sand photo
Antique white acrylic paint
Sandpaper
Envelope template to fit a
    6⅛ x 4⅝-inch card
Foam paintbrush
³⁄₁₆-inch-wide double-sided
    tape
Glue stick

Cut a 6⅛ x 9¼-inch piece of white card stock; score and fold in half. Glue a 6⅛ x 4⅝-inch piece of blue card stock to card front.

Trim photo to a 4⅜ x 3¼-inch rectangle; layer onto white card stock, trimming a small border. Glue in upper left corner of card. Attach a vacation-themed sticker in lower right corner of card. Glue "relax" definition in lower left corner, overlapping corner of photo. Transfer "leave it all behind" below definition.

Use foam paintbrush to apply a very light coat of antique white paint onto metal plaque. Let dry and adhere plaque in upper right corner of card using double-sided tape.

For envelope, use template to trace and cut an envelope from light brown card stock. Score and fold envelope flaps; adhere side and bottom flaps together. Lightly sand all edges. Attach vacation-themed stickers in lower left corner on front of envelope. ∎

SOURCES: Stickers, definition, metal feet plaque and rub-on transfer from Making Memories; envelope template from The C-Thru Ruler Co.

Beach Blast

Design by B A R B A R A   G R E V E

Adhere a 5 x 6½-inch piece of circle patterned paper to front of card. Cut a 4 x 5½-inch rectangle from summer-themed words patterned paper. Cut a 3¼ x 1-inch rectangle from vellum and a 1⅞ x ⅞-inch rectangle from scrap piece of white paper. Attach a reinforcement at each end of vellum rectangle; transfer "beach" across center of vellum rectangle.

Attach vellum rectangle across center of summer-themed word rectangle by using vellum tape at each end. Apply a dot of glue to the back of white paper and slip under vellum, highlighting word. Punch a ¼-inch hole through each hole reinforcement.

Cut two pieces of fiber, one 5 inches long and the other 12 inches long. Wrap and secure one end of short fiber inside the hole on right side of vellum rectangle; wrap and secure one end of long fiber inside the hole on left side of vellum rectangle. Center and glue assembled piece onto card.

Use paper piercer to pierce a hole through folded edge of card directly opposite from left hole in vellum rectangle. Insert long fiber through hole and wrap through card and around to front; tie into a knot with remaining end of short fiber. Trim ends and secure knot with glue.

Arrange and adhere stickers and dimensional heart embellishment onto card as desired. ■

SOURCES: Patterned papers and heart embellishment from KI Memories; stickers from EK Success; rub-on transfers from Scrapworks Inc.; Fabri-Tac adhesive from Beacon.

MATERIALS

5 x 6½-inch white card with yellow envelope
Coordinating summer-themed words and circle patterned papers
Clear vellum
Scrap piece of white paper
Beach-themed dimensional stickers
Round dimensional heart embellishment
Pink, orange and red letter rub-on transfers
Yellow and coral fibers
Pink and yellow self-adhesive reinforcements
¼-inch hole punch
Paper piercer
Glue pen
Permanent fabric adhesive
Vellum tape

Pool Party!

Design by TAMI MAYBERRY

MATERIALS

Turquoise striped double-
   sided card stock
Lime green card stock
Blue and lime green
   alphabet rub-on
   transfers
Blue acrylic rectangular tag
Blue fiber
Blue and lime green
   dimensional square
   stickers
Sunglasses button
Green mini brads
"You're Invited"
   rubber stamp
Blue ink pad
Envelope template to fit
   a 7 x 5-inch card
Button shank remover
Glue stick
Adhesive dots

Cut a 7 x 10-inch piece of striped double-sided card stock; score and fold in half. Transfer "it's a" at center top of card, near fold.

Transfer "pool" onto acrylic tag; remove shank from sunglasses button and attach button in lower right corner on tag with an adhesive dot. Thread fibers through each hole at top of tag. Lay tag on center of card front; extend fibers to upper corners of card and secure ends with mini brads. Secure tag with adhesive dots.

Transfer letters to spell "party" to square stickers; attach stickers at bottom of card.

For envelope, use envelope template to trace and cut an envelope from lime green card stock. Score and fold envelope flaps; adhere side and bottom flaps together.

Cut a 2 x 5-inch rectangle from striped double-sided card stock; glue along left edge of envelope, with striped side face up. Stamp "You're Invited" in blue ink onto striped rectangle. ∎

SOURCES: Double-sided card stock from Making Memories; rub-on transfers from Scrapworks Inc.; sunglasses button from Jesse James & Co. Inc.; square stickers from EK Success; acrylic tag from Heidi Grace Designs; rubber stamp from River City Rubber Works; Coluzzle envelope template from Provo Craft.

Treasures in the Sand

Design by SUSAN HUBER

Cut a 5½ x 8½-inch piece of card stock; score and fold in half. Cut three 5½ x 3¾-inch pieces of yellow patterned papers; tear each piece into a different size strip. Layer and adhere strips on front of card.

Die-cut four sand dollars from card stock; chalk edges and centers of sand dollars. Chalk card edges. Use adhesive foam tape to attach three sand dollars across center of card. Set four sand dollars aside for envelope.

Trim a 2½ x 1-inch rectangle from card stock; chalk edges. Cut a piece of "believe" ribbon; place ribbon across rectangle and punch a ¹⁄₁₆-inch hole at each end. Attach brads to hold ribbon in place. Wrap a piece of fiber around brad on right side. Attach rectangle to lower right corner of card with adhesive foam tape. Wrap fibers through card; tie a knot at top and trim ends.

Use envelope template to trace and cut an envelope from card stock. ***Note:*** *If desired, trim a wavy edge on top and bottom flaps.* Score and fold envelope flaps; glue side and bottom flaps together. Chalk edges.

Tear three small strips from patterned papers; layer and adhere to center of envelope. Tear another small strip from patterned paper and adhere to upper left corner on front of envelope. Glue remaining sand dollar to left side of envelope. ∎

SOURCES: Patterned papers and ribbon from Making Memories; Coluzzle envelope template from Provo Craft; sand dollar die and die-cutting tool from QuicKutz.

MATERIALS

Natural flecked card stock

3 coordinating yellow patterned papers

Die-cutting tool with sand dollar die

Golden brown chalk

Yellow fiber

Pale yellow "believe" printed ribbon

Mini round yellow brads

Envelope template to fit a 5½ x 4¼-inch card

¹⁄₁₆-inch hole punch

Adhesive foam tape

Glue stick

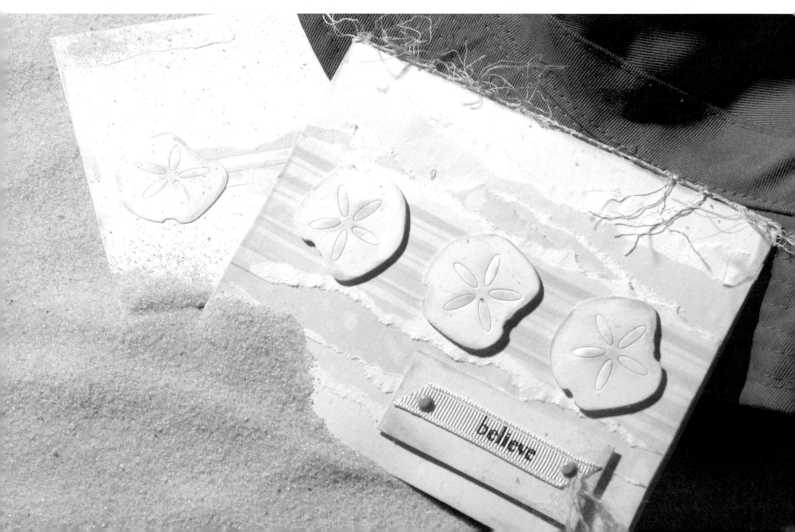

Refresh

Design by KATHLEEN PANEITZ

MATERIALS

Double-sided white/blue
    card stock
White card stock
Blue striped paper
Beach scene embossing
    template
White "refresh" rub-on
    transfer
Palm leaves and banana
    tree rub-on transfers
Chalk: blue, orange
2 turquoise round brads
Envelope template to fit a
    6⅜ x 4³⁄₁₆-inch card
Sandpaper
Embossing stylus
Light box or light source
Adhesive dots
Removable tape

Cut a 6⅜ x 8⅜-inch piece of white card stock; score and fold in half. Cut a 6⅜ x 4³⁄₁₆-inch piece of striped paper; glue to front of card.

Tape embossing template face down onto light source; place double-sided card stock on top of template, with blue side face down. Use stylus to emboss design onto card stock. Sand raised areas of design. Trim a rectangle around embossed design and adhere onto white card stock; trim a ¼-inch border.

Apply color to design with chalk. Transfer "refresh" along bottom edge of design; attach turquoise brads in upper left and lower right corners of design. Center and glue assembled piece onto card; transfer palm leaves in upper right and lower left corners of design.

For envelope, use envelope template to trace and cut an envelope from double-sided card stock with blue side on the outside of envelope. ***Note:*** *Template measurements may need to be adjusted slightly to fit card.* Score and fold envelope flaps, but do not adhere envelope together at this point.

Following previous embossing instructions, emboss desired portion from beach scene template onto left front side of envelope. Sand raised areas and along envelope folds. Adhere side and bottom flaps together. Transfer a banana tree next to chair. ∎

SOURCES: Double-sided card stock from Paper Adventures; striped paper from KI Memories; embossing template from Lasting Impressions for Paper Inc.; rub-on transfers from Making Memories and Duncan; envelope template from The C-Thru Ruler Co.

Near the Sea

Design by KATHLEEN PANEITZ

Score and fold a 5¼ x 7¾-inch piece of white card stock in half, forming a 5¼ x 3⅞-inch card. Cut a 5¼ x 3⅞-inch rectangle from blue card stock, a 5¼ x 3⅞-inch rectangle from transparency, a 4¼ x 3⅝-inch rectangle from olive green textured card stock and a 3½ x 3¼-inch rectangle from ivory card stock.

Transfer the lighthouse scene onto the ivory rectangle; layer ivory rectangle onto olive green rectangle and layer olive green rectangle onto blue rectangle.

Transfer sea-themed sentiment onto the center of transparency rectangle, leaving out a couple of words from sentiment. Fill in missing words with alphabet rub-on transfers.

Position transparency rectangle on top of layered rectangles; punch two ³⁄₁₆-inch holes on left side and attach washer eyelets. Thread ribbon through eyelets and tie a bow. Trim ribbon ends. Attach assembled piece onto card front.

To embellish envelope, transfer desired sea-themed motifs in lower left corner on front of envelope. ■

SOURCES: Washer eyelets from Creative Impressions; rub-on transfers from Duncan and Li'l Davis Designs.

MATERIALS
Card stock: white, blue textured, olive green textured and ivory
Transparency sheet
Rub-on transfers: sea-themed sentiment, green alphabet rectangles, lighthouse scene and assorted sea-themed motifs
³⁄₈-inch-wide green/blue plaid ribbon
White envelope to fit a 5¼ x 3⅞-inch card
Silver washer eyelets
³⁄₁₆-inch hole punch
Glue stick

Ocean Cruise

Design by L I N D A   B E E S O N

MATERIALS

Coordinating blue, gray and orange patterned papers

Coordinating gray tag with decorative corners

Blue and orange alphabet stickers

Dimensional stickers: suitcase, cruise ship and cruise-themed embellishments

"cruise" rub-on transfer

Black chalk ink pad

5/16-inch circle punch

Glue stick

Score and fold a 5½ x 11-inch piece of patterned paper in half, forming a 5½-inch square card. Ink edges. Attach alphabet stickers along upper left edge of card to spell "cruise."

Cut a 4-inch square and a 4¼-inch square from patterned papers. Use circle punch to punch a half circle from each corner of squares. Ink edges; layer and adhere squares on center of card.

Cut a ¼ x 4-inch strip of patterned paper; insert strip through hole in gray tag and carefully tie a loose knot. Trim strip ends. Ink edges of tag and glue to center of card.

Attach cruise ship and cruise-themed stickers to tag. Attach suitcase sticker in lower left corner of layered squares; attach "ocean" alphabet stickers along bottom edge of layered squares. Transfer "cruise" on top of "ocean." ■

SOURCES: Patterned papers, tag and alphabet stickers from Basic Grey; embellished stickers from Sandylion; chalk ink pad from Clearsnap; rub-on transfer from Making Memories.

By the Sea

Design by LINDA BEESON

Cut a 5½ x 3½-inch rectangle from tan card stock. Use turquoise ink to lightly stamp various postal symbols onto rectangle. Attach wave stickers in the lower left and upper right corners. Lightly sand stickers. Attach postal cancellation sticker in lower right corner.

Layer photo on turquoise card stock; trim edges with decorative-edge scissors. Referring to photo, glue layered photo to postcard. Transfer "enjoy" along left edge of postcard; transfer "4c" in lower right corner on top of sticker.

Stamp "by the sea" on left side of postcard with black ink; use black ink to stamp other postal images onto postcard, as desired. Rub brown chalk ink along edges of postcard. ∎

SOURCES: Stickers from Penny Black Inc. and EK Success; rubber stamps from Stampington & Co., Inkadinkado and Stampendous; rub-on transfers from Making Memories; chalk ink pad from Clearsnap.

MATERIALS

Card stock: tan, turquoise

Rubber stamps: alphabet, assorted postal symbols

Dye ink pads: black, turquoise

Brown chalk ink pad

Rub-on transfers: "enjoy," "4c"

Stickers: waves, postal cancellation symbol

Sandpaper

Decorative-edge scissors

Glue stick

Bon Voyage

Design by KATHLEEN PANIETZ

MATERIALS

Reproduction of vintage ship postcard

Pink and cream card stock

Desired sentiment

9 gold brads

Small round alphabet rub-on transfers

Rubber stamps: compass, Paris postmark and vintage "Post Card"

Black ink pad

Black fine-tip marker

Rounded corner punch

Double-sided adhesive sheets

Computer font (optional)

Round each corner of postcard with corner punch. Use a computer font or hand-print desired sentiment onto pink card stock; trim a rectangle around sentiment to fit across width of postcard. Adhere sentiment across bottom of postcard.

Stamp compass image in upper left corner of postcard; stamp Paris postmark in bottom left corner. Referring to photo, insert nine brads, separated into one grouping of three and one grouping of six, in top portion of postcard above ship. Transfer letters on each brad to spell "Bon Voyage."

Use a computer font or hand-print "Place Stamp Here" onto cream card stock; trim a 5⅛ x 3½-inch rectangle around words, positioning words in upper right corner of rectangle as for a postcard. Draw a square around words. Glue rectangle on reverse side of ship postcard. Round corners with corner punch to match up with postcard.

On cream side, stamp "Post Card" image in upper left corner. Draw a vertical line down center of postcard; draw four horizontal lines on right side of vertical line for address area. ∎

SOURCES: Postcard from me & my BIG ideas; rub-on transfers from Creative Imaginations; rubber stamps from Stampabilities.

Celebrate Freedom

Design by KAREN ROBINSON

Cut a 9¼ x 8-inch piece of blue card stock; score and fold in half. Cut two 9¼ x 1-inch strips from white card stock; cut a strip from red card stock the same size. Cut the long edges off diagonally on each strip, forming angled strips. Referring to photo, arrange and adhere strips to card. Machine-sew a zigzag stitch along horizontal edges of strips.

Use a computer font or hand-print "Freedom" across a piece of transparency at least 9¼ inches. Increase and decrease font sizes for each word. Option: Use black alphabet stickers instead of computer font. Trim transparency diagonally around words, forming a 9¼-inch-long angled strip. Repeat once to make an additional printed transparency strip. Place strips on top of white strips on card. Punch a ¹⁄₁₆-inch hole between each word and at each end; insert mini silver round brads to attach.

Use watermark ink to stamp "Celebrate!" in lower right corner on front of card; emboss with silver embossing powder.

For envelope, use template to trace and cut an envelope from white paper. Score and fold envelope flaps; glue side and bottom flaps together. Machine-sew a straight stitch around edge of top flap.

Punch two ¾-inch-diameter circles from red card stock; punch two 1-inch-diameter circles from blue card stock. Adhere red circles onto blue circles. Position one layered circle on top flap; punch a ¹⁄₁₆-inch hole in center and insert a star brad to secure. Position remaining layered circle below flap; punch a ¹⁄₁₆-inch hole through center of circle and insert a star brad to secure. Wrap silver cord around circles to close envelope.

SOURCES: Rubber stamp from Stampin' Up!; watermark ink pad from Tsukineko Inc.; star brads from Making Memories; envelope template from Deluxe Designs.

MATERIALS

Card stock: red, white
and blue
Transparency sheet
Medium-weight
white paper
"Celebrate" rubber stamp
Watermark ink pad
Silver embossing powder
Mini silver round brads
2 silver star brads
Silver cord
Envelope template to fit a
9¼ x 4-inch card
Sewing machine with silver
all-purpose thread
Circle punches: ¹⁄₁₆-,
¾- and 1-inch
Embossing heat tool
Glue stick
Computer font (optional)

MATERIALS

Beige and navy blue
    card stock
Red and beige striped
    patterned paper
Patriotic sheet music
    patterned paper
Stars and alphabet
    rubber stamps
Ink pads: brown, black
    solvent-based and
    embossing
Gold embossing powder
½-inch-wide ivory twill tape
2 metal rivets
Envelope template to fit a
    5-inch square card
Sandpaper
Embossing heat tool
Craft sponge
Glue stick
Double-sided tape
Computer font (optional)

Home of the Free

Design by SUSAN STRINGFELLOW

Score and fold a 10 x 5-inch piece of beige card stock in half, forming a 5-inch square card. Use craft sponge to apply brown ink to edges of card. Cut a 4½-inch square from navy blue card stock; sand edges. Sponge brown ink onto edges; center and glue onto card. Cut a 4⅛-inch square from striped patterned paper; center and glue to card.

Cut a 5-inch length of twill tape; use black solvent-based ink to stamp "home of the free and the brave" along length of twill tape. Lay twill down left side of card; attach at each end with rivets. If desired, secure twill tape with double-sided tape.

Use embossing ink to stamp stars randomly in lower right corner; emboss with gold embossing powder. Use a computer to print "4th" in reverse on the reverse side of navy blue card stock. ***Option:*** *Use number and alphabet templates to trace "4th" onto navy blue card stock.* Cut out number and letters; sand edges and sponge brown ink onto edges. Glue in lower right corner of card.

For envelope, use template to trace and cut an envelope from patriotic sheet music patterned paper; score and fold envelope flaps. Glue side and bottom flaps together.

Rub envelope edges with brown ink; use brown ink to stamp stars along left edge of envelope and onto right edge of top flap. ■

SOURCES: Patterned papers from Flair Designs; rubber stamp from Stampin' Up!; solvent-based ink pad from Tsukineko Inc.; rivets from Chatterbox Inc.; Coluzzle envelope template from Provo Craft.

Land of Liberty

Design by SANDRA GRAHAM SMITH

Score and fold a 10½ x 7½-inch piece of cream flecked card stock in half, forming a 5¼ x 7½-inch card. Adhere a 3½ x 7½-inch piece of brown star patterned paper to right side of card, lining up edges. Cut a 5 x 7½-inch piece of Statue of Liberty patterned paper, making sure to include the Statue of Liberty in piece; tear off right edge. Glue paper to left side of card, folding and adhering 1 inch of paper around folded card edge.

Punch seven stars from brown star patterned paper; set aside. Alternating between blue and red ink, stamp "AMERICA" onto cream flecked card stock. Cut out each letter and glue one letter to each punched star. Glue stars, evenly spaced, along left side of card. Attach a clear dimensional circle sticker on top of each letter.

For envelope, cut a 1½ x 5¼-inch strip from Statue of Liberty patterned paper and tear off right edge; cut a 1 x 5¼-inch strip from brown star patterned paper. Layer torn strip on top of brown star patterned strip and glue along left edge of envelope. ■

SOURCES: Patterned papers from Carolee's Creations & Company and Karen Foster Design; clear stickers from Making Memories; rubber stamps from River City Rubber Works.

MATERIALS

Brown star patterned
  paper
Statue of Liberty
  patterned paper
Cream flecked card stock
Cream envelope to fit a
  5¼ x 7½-inch card
Round alphabet
  rubber stamps
Blue and red ink pads
Clear dimensional
  circle stickers
Medium star punch
Glue stick

MATERIALS

Card stock: white glossy, red, white and blue
White paper
Blue rainbow and red rainbow ink pads
Rubber stamps: fireworks, checkered star, small star and alphabet
Blue metallic gel pen
Clear glitter glue
Envelope template to fit a 4¼ x 5½-inch card
Brush-tip markers
4-inch or smaller rubber brayer
Glue stick
Adhesive foam tape

Fireworks Celebration

Design by S U S A N H U B E R

Cut an 8½ x 5½-inch piece of red card stock; score and fold in half. Cut a 3⅞ x 5-inch rectangle from white glossy card stock; use rubber brayer to roll blue rainbow ink over top surface of rectangle. Once dry, cut rectangle into two pieces, one measuring 3⅞ x 3¾ inches and the other 3⅞ x 1¼ inches. Referring to photo, glue rectangles to card.

Use red and blue rainbow inks to randomly stamp fireworks onto a 3½ x 4½-inch piece of white glossy card stock. When dry, cut rectangle into two pieces, one measuring 3½ inches square and the other 3½ x 1 inch. Use blue rainbow ink to stamp "celebrate" onto the smaller piece; color letters in with blue metallic gel pen. Layer each stamped piece onto red card stock; trim a small border on each and referring to photo, glue to card.

Stamp several checkered stars onto white glossy card stock with blue and red rainbow inks; cut out each star and layer onto red or blue card stock, trimming a small border. Attach stars randomly to the front of the card with adhesive foam tape. Apply glitter glue to stars and fireworks. Trim star edges extending past edge of card.

For inside the card, cut a 2⅞ x 3½-inch rectangle from white paper. Stamp "Have a Happy and Safe Fourth of July!" onto rectangle; outline edge of rectangle with gel pen. Glue rectangle inside card. Stamp small stars randomly around sentiment.

Use envelope template to trace and cut an envelope from white card stock. Score and fold envelope flaps; glue side and bottom flaps together. Color fireworks stamps with markers and stamp onto left side of envelope; accent fireworks with glitter glue. ∎

SOURCES: Kaleidacolor ink pads from Tsukineko Inc.; alphabet rubber stamps from Stampin' Up!; Coluzzle envelope template from Provo Craft.

Patriotic Picnic Invitation

Design by TAMI MAYBERRY

Cut a 7 x 10-inch piece of dark red card stock; cut a 6½ x 9½-inch piece of plaid patterned paper. Center and adhere plaid patterned paper to dark red card stock; score and fold in half.

Cut a 2 x 2½-inch piece of dark red card stock and adhere in upper left corner of card. Cut a ½ x 2⅜-inch piece of dark red card stock; adhere piece onto the right edge of a 5 x 3-inch piece of navy blue card stock. Referring to photo, adhere navy blue piece onto card, overlapping first dark red piece. Transfer "FREEDOM" onto navy blue piece, "picnic" on small dark red piece and "July 4" onto first dark red piece.

Use mini adhesive dots to attach alphabet beads below "FREEDOM" to spell "Celebration." Thread star buttons, evenly spaced, onto white fiber; position fiber across bottom of card. Attach fiber ends to card with mini brads; secure buttons with mini adhesive dots.

Use envelope template to trace and cut an envelope from navy blue card stock; score and fold envelope flaps. Glue side and bottom flaps together. ■

SOURCES: Rub-on transfers from Making Memories and Royal & Langnickel; star buttons from Junkitz; Coluzzle envelope template from Provo Craft.

MATERIALS

Dark red and navy blue card stock
Red and blue plaid patterned paper
Patriotic-themed words rub-on transfers
White alphabet rub-on transfers
White alphabet beads
Dark red mini brads
Red, clear and blue star buttons
White fiber
Envelope template to fit a 7 x 5-inch card
Mini adhesive dots
Glue stick

Teacher Appreciation

Design by SHERRY WRIGHT

MATERIALS

Card stock: light brown

Printed papers: lined
    school writing paper,
    alphabet and ruler
    print, map print

Manila library pocket

Initial stencil: "A"

Sticker: red plaid border

Metal word: "wisdom"

2 bottle caps

2 silver mini round brads

Rub-on transfers: star, heart

Brown antique-finish
    ink pad

Envelope template to fit a
    6-inch square card

Label maker with black
    label tape

1/16-inch hole punch

Hammer

Adhesive dots

Paper adhesive

Cut a 6 x 12-inch piece of light brown card stock; score and fold in half. Center and glue a 5¾-inch square piece of lined school writing paper to card front.

Cut a 6 x 1-inch strip from alphabet portion of printed paper; cut a 6 x 9/16-inch strip from ruler portion of printed paper. Referring to photo for placement, glue strips, evenly spaced, to bottom portion of card. Attach red plaid border sticker to top edge of card; trim edges evenly with card.

Cut a 2-inch square piece of map print paper; position square in a diamond shape and glue to left side of card. Ink stencil. Cut small pieces from red plaid border sticker and ruler portion of printed paper; glue to edges of initial stencil as desired. Punch two 1/16-inch holes through bottom edge of stencil; insert brads. Glue stencil to diamond shape on card.

Using label maker, make a label spelling "PPRECIATION"; attach beside stencil. Cut out "i" and "n" from alphabet print paper; glue above "Appreciation" to complete sentiment.

Hammer a bottle cap slightly; ink bottle cap. Transfer a star rub-on to center of bottle cap; ink again. Use adhesive dots to attach bottle cap to lower right corner of card.

For inside card, cut a 6 x 5½-inch piece from alphabet portion of printed paper; glue inside card, lining up top edge with center fold. Cut a 5 x 2-inch rectangle from map print paper; glue to bottom right edge. Glue a 2½ x 5½-inch piece of lined school writing paper to left side.

Cut scraps from printed papers and glue to library pocket as desired. Hammer another bottle cap slightly; ink bottle cap and transfer a heart rub-on to center. Glue metal word to library pocket; use adhesive dots to attach bottle cap to pocket.

For envelope, use template to trace and cut an envelope from lined school writing paper; score and fold envelope flaps. Glue side and bottom flaps together. Ink edges. Cut various size strips from ruler and alphabet portions of printed paper; glue pieces to envelope as desired. ■

SOURCES: Printed papers from Making Memories, K&Company and Scenic Route Paper Co.; sticker from Pebbles Inc.; metal word from Darice Inc.; rub-on transfers from Li'l Davis Designs; template from Green Sneakers Inc.

Thanks a Latte

Design by KATHLEEN PANEITZ

Cut an 8 x 5½-inch piece of blue card stock; score and fold in half. Cut a 4 x 5⅜-inch piece of red distressed paper; sand edges. Cut a 1⅝ x 5⅜-inch piece of ruler print paper. Lay ruler print paper on left side of red distressed paper; using sewing machine, zigzag stitch along left and right edges of ruler print paper.

Stamp coffee-cup image onto fabric pocket; color image with chalks. Use rub-on transfers to add "thanks a latte!" to pocket. Use double-sided tape and staples to attach pocket to assembled piece of paper. Center and glue assembled piece to card front. Slide gift card in pocket.

For envelope, use template to trace and cut an envelope from light tan card stock. Score and fold envelope flaps; glue side and bottom flaps together. Sand edges. Stamp coffee-cup image in lower left corner on front of envelope. Color image with chalks. ■

SOURCES: Printed papers from 7gypsies; rubber stamp from Magenta; fabric pocket, staples and rub-on transfers from Making Memories.

MATERIALS

Card stock: blue, light tan
Printed papers: ruler print, red distressed
Light tan fabric pocket
Black alphabet rub-on transfers
Coffee cup rubber stamp
Black dye ink pad
Chalk
Coffee shop gift card
Envelope template to fit a 4 x 5½-inch card
Sandpaper
Stapler with blue staples
Sewing machine with blue all-purpose thread
Glue stick
Double-sided tape

Great Teacher

Design by LORETTA MATEIK

MATERIALS

Card stock: pale yellow, black
Rubber stamps: "thanks," small moon with stars, desired sentiment
White envelope to fit a 4¼ x 5½-inch card
Black dye ink pad
⅝-inch-wide sheer black ribbon
Magnet sheet
Craft knife
Paper adhesive
Computer font (optional)

Cut an 8½ x 5½-inch piece of pale yellow card stock; score and fold in half. Open card and using a craft knife, cut a 2½6 x 1¹³⁄₁₆-inch window from center of card front ⅛ inch from bottom edge.

Use a computer to generate, or hand-print, "To a Great Teacher" on pale yellow card stock; trim a 1½ x 2¼-inch rectangle around words. Cut a 1½ x ⅝-inch rectangle from pale yellow card stock; stamp "thanks" on rectangle. Cut a 2½ x 3¼-inch rectangle from black card stock. Referring to photo, glue both pale yellow rectangles to black rectangle. Glue to card, centering it above window. Stamp desired sentiment inside card, positioning it so it can be seen through window.

Stamp same sentiment on pale yellow card stock; trim a 1¾ x 1½-inch rectangle around sentiment and layer on black card stock. Trim a small border. Stamp moon with stars image on pale yellow card stock; trim a rectangle around image the same size as pale yellow rectangle above. Layer on black card stock and trim a small border.

Cut two pieces from magnet sheet the same size as layered rectangles. Cut a 10-inch length of ribbon; place one ribbon end on reverse side of a layered rectangle. Glue one magnet to layered rectangle, securing ribbon end in between. Repeat for other ribbon end with remaining magnet and layered rectangle, forming a bookmark.

Place either end of bookmark inside card, positioning it so it can be seen through window; wrap ribbon around top edge of card and place bottom rectangle toward bottom of card. The magnets will connect and secure the bookmark to the card.

To decorate envelope, stamp moon with stars image in lower left corner on front of envelope; stamp "thanks" above moon with stars. ■

SOURCE: Rubber stamps from Stampin' Up!.

Best Teacher

Design by ANGELIA WIGGINTON

MATERIALS

Printed card stock: tan
   distressed-looking,
   light burgundy motif
Coordinating printed tags:
   small round, large
Ivory envelope to fit a
   5 x 4⅛-inch card
Rub on transfer:
   "gratitude"
Stickers: "Best," "teacher"
2 decorative brads
⅝-inch-wide white with
   black polka-dots ribbon
Sandpaper
Hole punches: ⅛- and
   ¼-inch
Glue stick

Cut a 10 x 4⅛-inch rectangle from tan printed card stock; score and fold in half. Lightly sand edges of card and both tags. With prepunched hole on left side, punch a ⅛-inch hole through right side of round tag; insert brad. Referring to photo for placement, glue tags to card front, positioning round tag on the left side of card, overlapping large tag. *Note: If needed, trim end of large tag to fit card.*

Attach "Best" and "teacher" stickers to large tag; transfer "gratitude" rub-on to round tag, positioning it vertically. Punch a ¼-inch hole through prepunched hole in tags. Thread ribbon through hole and tie a knot. Trim ends.

For envelope, use top envelope flap on ivory envelope to trace and cut an envelope flap from light burgundy motif card stock. Glue printed flap to envelope; lightly sand edges. Punch a ¼-inch hole through bottom center of envelope flap; insert brad.

SOURCES: Printed card stock and tags from BasicGrey; brads and rub-on transfer from Making Memories; stickers from me & my BIG ideas and Deluxe Designs.

Back to School

Design by KATHLEEN PANEITZ

MATERIALS

Card stock: white, tan, red

Printed paper: blue with
    alphabet print

Alphabet print twill ribbon

"Back to School" tag

Rub-on transfers:
    alphabet, numbers

Apple rubber stamp

Acrylic paint: tan, green, red

Brown antique-finish
    ink pad

White string

Envelope template to fit a
    4-inch square card

Bleach

Sandpaper

Foam brush

Glue stick

Double-sided tape

Cut a 4 x 8-inch piece of tan card stock; score and fold in half. Cut a 3¾-inch square from printed paper; sand edges and glue to card front.

Cut two 3¾-inch pieces of twill ribbon; use double-sided tape to attach one piece ¾ inch below top edge of card. Attach remaining piece ¾ inch above bottom edge.

Use acrylic paints to stamp apple image on white card stock. Let dry. Trim a small border around apple; ink apple with brown ink. Using rub-ons, transfer "1," "2" and "3" onto apple.

Transfer desired year onto "Back to School" tag; ink tag with brown ink. Thread string through hole in tag and tie to stem on apple; knot ends and trim. Glue assembled piece to center of card front.

For envelope, use template to trace and cut an envelope from red card stock. Score and fold envelope flaps; glue side and bottom flaps together.

Cut two 4¼ x ½-inch strips from printed paper; sand edges. Glue one strip along top edge of envelope front; glue remaining strip along bottom edge.

Dip apple stamp in a small amount of bleach; stamp image on lower left corner of envelope. Let dry. ***Note:*** *Rinse stamp in water immediately so bleach does not damage rubber.* Transfer "A," "B" and "C" onto apple image. ■

SOURCES: Printed paper from 7gypsies; twill ribbon from Creative Impressions; rubber stamp from Duncan; tag from Making Memories; ink pad from Ranger; rub-on transfers from Autumn Leaves; template from The C-Thru Ruler Co.

Treasured Teacher

Design by TAMI MAYBERRY

MATERIALS

Card stock: burgundy,
olive green
Printed papers: acorn,
burgundy canvas print
Metal tags: "teacher,"
"Treasure"
Rub-on transfers:
"A," "Special"
Acorn rubber stamp
Brown antique-finish
ink pad
¼-inch-wide brown
gingham ribbon
Envelope template to fit
a 6 x 4-inch card
1½-inch square punch
Paper adhesive

Cut a 12 x 4-inch piece of burgundy card stock; score and fold in half, forming a 6 x 4-inch card. Punch four 1½-inch squares each from olive green card stock and acorn print paper. Cut a 4½ x 1½-inch piece of olive green card stock; tear off top and bottom edges. Ink edges on all pieces.

Using rub-ons, transfer "A" and "Special" to torn piece, positioning words in center. Glue piece to lower right corner of card, lining up right edges. Glue "Treasure" tag to piece, positioning it after "Special."

Referring to photo, adhere squares randomly to card. Thread ribbon through "teacher" tag; glue tag to center of card. Glue ribbon to card; trim ends evenly with card.

Use envelope template to trace and cut an envelope from burgundy print paper; score and fold envelope flaps. Glue side and bottom flaps together. Stamp acorn image in lower left corner on front of envelope. ■

SOURCES: Printed papers from The C-Thru Ruler Co. and Karen Foster Design; metal tags from Karen Foster Design and All My Memories; rub-on transfers from Junkitz; rubber stamp from Close To My Heart; ink pad from Ranger.

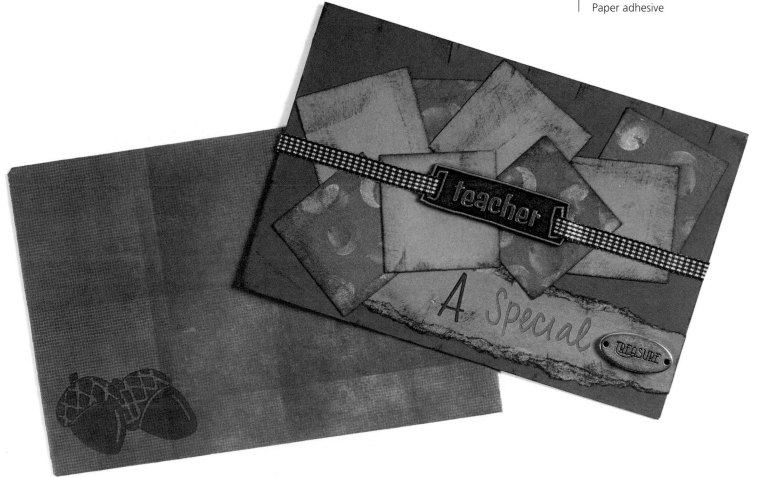

MATERIALS

Card stock: sage green, red, yellow, cream
Printed paper: red school-theme, white with green alphabet
Wooden shapes: apple, "A+"
Acrylic paint: dark green, off-white, light brown
Rub-on transfers: black alphabet, small apple
School bus rubber stamp
Pigment ink pads: brown, black
Clear embossing powder
Red pen
⅝-inch-wide black gingham ribbon
Envelope template to fit a 4¼-inch square card
Magnet strip
Sandpaper
Craft sponge
Paintbrush
Embossing heat tool
Sewing machine with red all-purpose thread
Hook-and-loop tape
Decoupage medium
Paper adhesive

Apple for Teacher

Design by KATHLEEN PANEITZ

Cut an 8½ x 4¼-inch piece of sage green card stock; score and fold in half. Center and glue a 3¾ x 4-inch piece of alphabet print paper to card. Using sewing machine, zigzag stitch around edge of alphabet print paper.

Cut a 5-inch length of ribbon; tie a knot in center. Referring to photo for placement, glue knot to center bottom portion of card.

Paint reverse side of wooden apple, side edges and stem dark green; let dry. Cut a piece of red school-theme print paper to cover top surface of apple, except for stem; glue paper to apple. Trim edges evenly around apple. Sand edges. Paint wooden "A+" off-white; let dry. Dab light brown paint on edges with a dry sponge.

Using black ink, stamp school bus image on yellow card stock. Sprinkle image with clear embossing powder and emboss. Color window edges and school bus lights with red pen. Glue school bus to red side of wooden apple.

Using rub-ons, transfer "teacher" to top portion of apple. Glue "A+" to bottom portion of apple. Apply a thin coat of decoupage medium to apple; let dry thoroughly. Glue magnet strip to reverse side of apple.

Attach one piece of hook-and-loop tape to card; attach other half of hook-and-loop tape to wooden apple. Connect hook-and-loop pieces together to attach apple magnet to card.

For envelope, use template to trace and cut an envelope from red card stock. Score and fold envelope flaps; sand edges. Before assembling envelope, cut a 1¼ x 4½-inch piece of alphabet print paper; use sewing machine to zigzag stitch the piece to what will be the left side of envelope front. Glue side and bottom flaps together to assemble.

Transfer an apple image to cream card stock; cut a 1¼ x 1⅜-inch rectangle around apple. Ink edges with brown ink. Glue rectangle to sage green card stock; trim a small border. Glue layered piece to front of envelope, overlapping bottom portion of alphabet print paper strip. ∎

SOURCES: Printed papers from KI Memories and 7gypsies; rubber stamp from Delta/Rubber Stampede; wooden apple from Plaid; rub-on transfers from KI Memories; template from The C-Thru Ruler Co.

Leaves in the Window

Design by MARY AYRES

Cut a 10 x 7-inch piece of brown card stock; score and fold in half. Ink edges. Center and glue a 4 x 6-inch piece of dark purple card stock to card front.

Varying their sizes, cut one rectangle each from pale yellow, pale mint green, ivory and light orange card stock; cut two rectangles from light gray card stock. Stamp mesh texture image on each rectangle; ink rectangle edges. Set ivory and one light gray rectangle aside. Referring to photo for placement, glue remaining four rectangles to card front, leaving center right portion of dark purple rectangle empty.

Attach a leaf sticker to each rectangle; punch a ¹⁄₁₆-inch hole through each rectangle corner; insert brads.

Cut a 1¾ x 2¼-inch rectangle from gray card stock; ink edges. Glue rectangle to empty portion of dark purple rectangle on card. Using a craft knife, cut a 1⅜ x 1⅞-inch window from center of gray rectangle; ink interior edges of window.

Cut a 2 x 2½-inch rectangle from dark purple card stock; glue stamped ivory rectangle to dark purple rectangle. Glue layered rectangle inside card, positioning it so it shows through window. Attach a leaf sticker to layered rectangle inside card.

For envelope, glue remaining light gray rectangle to gray card stock. Trim a small border. Ink edges. Attach a leaf sticker to center of layered rectangle. Glue rectangle to top envelope flap. ∎

SOURCES: Stickers from Frances Meyer Inc.; Aleene's Memory Glue from Duncan.

MATERIALS

Card stock: dark purple, brown, ivory, light gray, gray, pale mint green, light orange, pale yellow

Yellow-orange envelope to fit a 5 x 7-inch card

Autumn leaf stickers

Mesh texture rubber stamp

Brown dye ink pad

4 ivory mini round brads

¹⁄₁₆-inch hole punch

Paper adhesive

Beribboned Elegance

Design by JEANNE WYNHOFF

MATERIALS

Card stock: burgundy

Printed paper: burgundy distressed-looking

Ribbons: ⅝-inch-wide burgundy grosgrain, 2½-inch-wide sheer burgundy autumn leaf print

Burgundy chalk ink pad

Envelope template to fit a 5½ x 4¼-inch card

Stapler with staples

Adhesive applicator with permanent adhesive cartridges

Dimensional adhesive dots

Glue stick

Cut a 5½ x 8½-inch piece of burgundy card stock; score and fold in half. Ink edges. Cut a 4¾ x 4-inch piece of printed paper; tear off left and bottom edges. Ink edges of printed paper; glue to card, positioning straight edges next to top and right edges of card.

Cut a 4¾-inch length of sheer ribbon; run ribbon through adhesive applicator. Attach ribbon to right side of card, wrapping and adhering ends inside card and on reverse side of card.

Cut a 4-inch length of sheer ribbon that includes two autumn motifs; run ribbon through adhesive applicator. Cut out two autumn motifs from ribbon; attach both to burgundy card stock. Trim around motifs. Use dimensional adhesive dots to attach autumn motifs to card front, referring to photo for placement.

Cut three 2-inch lengths of grosgrain ribbon; cut ribbon ends at an angle. Fold each piece in half and staple them to the left side of the card. Glue a 5⅜ x 4⅛-inch piece of burgundy card stock inside card on reverse side of card front to cover staples and ribbon end.

For envelope, use template to trace an envelope on the reverse side of printed paper. Cut out envelope; score and fold envelope flaps. Glue side and bottom flaps together. Ink edges.

Cut a piece of sheer ribbon that includes an autumn motif; run ribbon through adhesive applicator. Cut out autumn motif; attach motif to burgundy card stock. Trim motif. Glue motif to lower left corner on front of envelope. ■

SOURCES: Printed paper from Karen Foster Design; ink pad from Clearsnap Inc.; template from Duncan; adhesive applicator and cartridges from Xyron.

Changing Seasons

Design by KATHLEEN PANEITZ

Cut an 8½ x 5½-inch piece of brown card stock; score and fold in half. Center and glue a 4³⁄₁₆ x 5³⁄₁₆-inch piece of harlequin print paper to card front. Cut a 2⅜ x 2⅝-inch piece of dark brown card stock; ink edges. Center and glue to card.

Condition clay by kneading it with hands until it is warm and pliable. Roll out clay on work surface to a thin sheet approximately ⅛ inch thickness; slide clay into tree punch and punch out shape. Following manufacturer's instructions, bake clay tree. Let piece cool. Use mini adhesive dots to attached cooled tree to card.

Using mini leaf punch, punch a few leaves from scrap pieces of card stock. Use mini adhesive dots to attach mini leaves to tree.

Using fingers, apply off-white paint to metal embellishment; wipe off excess with paper towels. Referring to photo, glue embellishment to card, overlapping bottom of tree.

For envelope, use template to trace and cut an envelope from printed paper. Score and fold envelope flaps; glue side and bottom flaps together.

Cut a 2⅛ x 2⅜-inch rectangle from dark brown card stock. Dip leaf stamp into a small amount of bleach; stamp image on dark brown rectangle. Let dry. Ink edges. Glue rectangle to lower left corner on envelope front. ■

SOURCES: Printed paper from Scenic Route Paper Co.; punches from EK Success and Plaid/All Night Media; clay from Polyform Products Co.; metal embellishment from Making Memories; rubber stamp from Duncan; template from The C-Thru Ruler Co.

MATERIALS

Card stock: brown, dark brown, scrap pieces of red, olive green and pale orange
Printed paper: reddish-brown harlequin print
Translucent polymer clay
Metal embellishment: "changing seasons"
Maple leaf rubber stamp
White dye ink pad
Off-white acrylic paint
Bleach
Paper towels
Envelope template to fit a 4½ x 5½-inch card
Punches: mini leaf, tree
Acrylic clay roller *or* brayer
Mini adhesive dots
Paper adhesive

Shades of Autumn

Design by KATHLEEN PANEITZ

MATERIALS

Cream card stock

Printed paper: brown autumn-theme text

Gourd and pumpkin autumn-theme rubber stamp

Ink pads: light brown antique-finish, brown dye

Chalk, desired colors

Ribbon: brown "autumn splendor" print

Red fine-tip marker

Envelope template to fit a 7⅛ x 4⅛-inch card

Spray sealer

Double-sided tape

Glue stick

Cut a 7⅛ x 8¼-inch piece of cream card stock; score and fold in half, forming a 7⅛ x 4⅛-inch card. Cut a 6⅞ x 3⅞-inch piece of printed paper; set aside. Using brown dye ink, stamp autumn-theme image on cream card stock. Color image with marker and chalk; spray with sealer. Let dry. Inking directly to card stock, drag light brown ink pad horizontally across image; repeat, dragging ink pad vertically across image. Trim a 3⅞ x 3¼-inch rectangle around image. Ink edges with light brown ink. Center and glue to printed paper piece.

Wrap ribbon around left side of paper; tie a knot and trim ends. Secure ribbon with double-sided tape. Glue assembled piece to card front.

For envelope, drag light brown ink pad across a sheet of cream card stock. Use template to trace and cut an envelope from inked card stock; score and fold envelope flaps. Glue side and bottom flaps together.

Use brown ink to stamp autumn-theme image to lower left corner on front of envelope. Color with marker and chalk; spray with sealer. ■

SOURCES: Printed paper from Daisy D's Paper Co.; rubber stamp from Duncan; ribbon from Creative Impressions; ink pads from Ranger; spray sealer from Krylon.

Leaf Sampler

Design by BARBARA GREVE

Cut a 5 x 6-inch piece of brown printed paper. Cut a ⅞ x 5½-inch strip of ivory crackle paper; glue along left edge of brown paper. Using large rub-ons, transfer "FALLING" to strip.

Cut four varying size rectangles from ivory crackle paper; arrange and glue to paper as desired. Using paper piercer, pierce three holes in one rectangle; attach leaf brads. Use sewing needle and orange or black embroidery floss to sew buttons and charms to remaining rectangles, piercing holes as needed. Use photo as a reference.

Thread a charm on sheer ribbon; staple to top of paper and trim ribbon ends. Pierce two holes next to each other on paper where desired; thread black embroidery floss through holes and tie on a charm. Tie a knot on front; trim ends.

Use small rub-ons to transfer the letters for "leaves" on small tag stickers; carefully thread stickers on fiber. Attach fiber and tags to card where desired. Attach two tag stickers to paper as desired; pierce a hole through each tag holes and insert brads.

For envelope, carefully take apart premade envelope and use as a template to trace and cut an envelope from ivory crackle paper. Score and fold envelope flaps; glue side and bottom flaps together.

Place a leaf button on center bottom edge of top envelope flap; pierce holes through button holes. Use sewing needle and ivory embroidery floss to sew button on flap; knot ends inside and trim excess. Repeat to sew another button directly below center of envelope flap.

Cut an 8-inch length of embroidery floss; sew one end of length underneath top leaf button on envelope flap. Let remaining length hang to loop around buttons to secure envelope closed. Knot end of floss. ■

SOURCES: Brown printed paper from 7gypsies; buttons and charms from Junkitz and Doodlebug Design Inc.; rub-on transfers from Making Memories and Doodlebug Design Inc.; stickers from Doodlebug Design Inc; adhesive from Decorator's Solution.

MATERIALS

5 x 6-inch white card

Envelope to fit a 5 x 6-inch card

Printed papers: brown, ivory crackle

Small orange and yellow card-stock tag stickers

Rub-on transfers: large and small black alphabets

Leaf buttons

Assorted leaf charms

Brads: 2 brass round, 3 leaves

¼-inch-wide sheer brown ribbon

Black, ivory and orange embroidery floss

Beige fiber

Stapler with staples

Sewing needle

Paper piercer

Paper adhesive

Touch of Elegance DIAGRAMS ON PAGE 153

Design by SHARON REINHART

MATERIALS

Dark green card stock

Metallic papers: copper,
    dark green, brown

Transparency sheet

White mat board

Punches: scallop-edge
    square, medium leaf

Autumn leaf background
    rubber stamp

Ink pads: watermark, olive
    green solvent-based

Japan threads: copper, gold

Copper leafing pen

Leaf button

Button shank remover

Cellophane tape

Mini adhesive dots

Glue stick

Cut an 11 x 4¼-inch piece of dark green card stock; score and fold in half. Use watermark ink to stamp autumn leaf background on card front; let dry. Referring to photo for placement, punch a scallop-edge square from the right side of card front approximately ⅝ inch from right edge. Set aside punched square.

Cut a 2¾-inch square from transparency sheet. Use olive green ink to stamp autumn leaf background on transparency square; let dry. Use cellophane tape to attach stamped transparency to reverse side of opening.

Cut a 5⅜ x 4⅛-inch rectangle from copper metallic paper; glue inside card on reverse side of card front. *Note: Do not apply adhesive to area that will show through transparency.*

Cut a 65-inch length of copper thread. Holding punched scallop-edge square in a diamond shape position, tape end of thread to upper right reverse side. Referring to Fig. 1 on page 153, wrap thread around to front side, placing thread in the first scallop mark to the right of top scallop; wrap thread across diamond and place thread in the first bottom scallop mark to the left of bottom scallop. Wrap thread around to reverse side and place thread in second scallop mark; wrap thread across diamond and place thread in the second bottom scallop mark. Dashed lines on figures refer to thread on reverse side of diamond. In same manner, continue wrapping thread in a clockwise manner until complete; tape end of thread to reverse side. Trim excess.

Cut an 82-inch length of gold thread; tape end of thread to upper right reverse side. In same manner as above and referring to Fig. 2 on page 153, wrap thread around to front side and place in first scallop mark; wrap thread across diamond and place thread in first bottom scallop mark to the left of bottom scallop. Repeat once. Bring thread up to scallop mark on left side of top scallop and wrap across to first bottom scallop mark on right side; repeat once. Tape end of thread to reverse side; trim excess. Rotate diamond shape ¼ turn and repeat.

Cut a 2-inch square from mat board; color edges of square with copper leafing pen. Glue to reverse side of embellished scallop-edge square. Referring to photo for placement, glue to left side of card. Color button with leafing pen; let dry. Remove button shank; use an adhesive dot to attach button to center of assembled scallop-edge square on card.

Punch three leaves each from copper, dark green and brown metallic papers. Glue three leaves overlapping to right side of card, overlapping transparency. Glue remaining leaves randomly to card. For envelope, punch additional leaves from metallic papers and glue to left side of envelope. ∎

SOURCES: Rubber stamp from Plaid/All Night Media; ink pads from Tsukineko Inc.; punches from Uchida of America and McGill Inc.; Japan threads from Kreinik; leafing pen from Krylon.

Autumn Splendor

Design by S U S A N   H U B E R

Cut a 5½ x 8½-inch piece of yellow card stock; score and fold in half. Center and glue a 5⅛ x 3⅞-inch piece of orange card stock to card front. Transfer leaf motifs to upper corners of card.

Attach photo sticker to orange card stock; trim a small border. Center and glue to card. Use craft knife to cut a ½-inch-long slit in top fold of card ¾ inch from right edge. Thread ribbon through slit and knot ends together on card front; trim ends. Transfer "Leaves" rub-on to lower right corner of card, overlapping ribbon.

Rub green and brown ink on cork leaf; glue to lower left corner of card.

For envelope, use template to trace and cut an envelope from gold vellum; score and fold envelope flaps. Glue side and bottom flaps together. Transfer desired leaf motif on lower left corner of front. ∎

SOURCES: Sticker from Pebbles Inc.; cork leaf from LazerLetterz; ink pads from Ranger; rub-on transfers from Wordsworth Art Stamps; template from Lasting Impressions for Paper Inc.

MATERIALS

Card stock: yellow, orange

Gold vellum

Autumn leaf photo sticker

Rub-on transfers: "Leaves", assorted leaf motifs

Cork leaf

Antique-finish ink pads: green, brown

⅜-inch-wide sage green ribbon

Envelope template to fit a 5½ x 4¼-inch card

Craft knife

Paper adhesive

Fall Colors DIAGRAM ON PAGE 153

Design by MARY AYRES

MATERIALS

Card stock: light brown,
   brown, black, metallic
   gold and four shades
   of yellow/orange
Coordinating envelope to
   fit a 7 x 5-inch card
White vellum
Computer photo paper
Photo of autumn leaves
Brown ink pad
2 gold mini round brads
¹⁄₁₆-inch hole punch
Spray sealer
Paper adhesive
Computer with scanner,
   printer and photo
   editing software

Cut a 7 x 10-inch piece of brown card stock; score and fold in half. Ink edges. Center and glue a 6½ x 4½-inch piece of black card stock to card front.

Cut a 6¼ x 4¼-inch piece of light brown card stock; ink edges and glue to card. Using pattern provided, trace and cut two corners from metallic gold card stock; glue metallic gold corners to lower left and upper right corners of light brown rectangle on card, lining up straight edges.

Using computer and scanner, scan leaf photo and print two copies on photo paper; trim each image to 2½ x 3³⁄₁₆ inches. Ink edges; set aside one image to be used later on envelope.

Using computer and photo editing software, change photo image to black and white. Print black and white image on the four varying shades of yellow/orange card stocks. Trim each image to the same size as the first colored photo image. Referring to photo, overlap and adhere printed images to card, with colored image on top in lower right corner.

Use a computer to generate, or hand-print, "Beautiful Fall Foliage" on vellum; spray words with sealer to set ink. Tear a 5½ x 1-inch rectangle around words; place rectangle on card, referring to photo for placement. Punch a ¹⁄₁₆-inch hole on each end of vellum rectangle; insert brads.

For envelope, cut a 1¼ x 5¾-inch strip of light brown card stock; ink edges. Glue strip to left side of envelope. Glue remaining colored photo image to black card stock; trim a small border and glue to upper left corner of envelope, overlapping light brown strip. ∎

SOURCES: Spray sealer from Krylon; paper adhesive from Decorator's Solution.

Framed Leaf

Design by KATHLEEN PANEITZ

Cut a 5½ x 8½-inch piece of brown card stock; score and fold in half. Trim photo to 5¼ x 4 inches; center and attach to card with double-sided tape. Punch a 1¾-inch square opening in lower right corner on front of card.

Use paper adhesive to attach leather frame over opening. Cut a 3 x 2½-inch piece of blue mesh; attach inside card, positioning it so it shows through opening. Attach leaf sticker to mesh, positioning it so it shows through opening.

For envelope, use template to trace and cut an envelope from yellow card stock. Score and fold envelope flaps; glue side and bottom flaps together. Stamp three leaf images in lower left corner on front of envelope; stamp one leaf on reverse side of envelope. ∎

SOURCES: Frame from Making Memories; sticker from Colorbök; mesh from Magic Mesh; rubber stamp from Duncan; template from The C-Thru Ruler Co.

MATERIALS

Card stock: brown, yellow
Autumn leaf photo
Small brown leather frame
Self-adhesive blue mesh
Dimensional leaf sticker
Leaf rubber stamp
Brown ink pad
Envelope template to fit a
    5½ x 4¼-inch card
1¾-inch square punch
Double-sided tape
Paper adhesive

Autumn Magic

Design by CAMI BAUMAN

MATERIALS

Card stock: brown,
    ivory, orange
Shrink plastic
Printed paper: gold leaves
4¾ x 7-inch ivory card
    with envelope
Leaf stamp
Ink pads: golden yellow,
    yellow, brown, dark
    brown, tan
Ribbons: 1½-inch-wide
    gold wired, ⅜-inch-
    wide multicolored
Heat embossing tool
Adhesive dots
Tape
Double-sided tape
Glue stick
Computer fonts (optional)

Cut a 4¾ x 7-inch piece of brown card stock; glue to front of ivory card. Center and glue a 4⁵⁄₁₆ x 6½-inch piece of orange card stock to card front.

Use a computer to generate, or hand-print, desired autumn-theme poem on gold leaves printed paper; trim a 4 x 6¼-inch rectangle around poem, positioning poem at bottom of rectangle. Ink edges with brown ink.

Cut a 5-inch length of wired gold ribbon; glue ribbon 1 inch from top edge of gold leaves printed paper; wrap and tape ends to reverse side. Cut a 5-inch length of multicolored ribbon; center and glue to wired ribbon. Wrap and tape ends to reverse side. Glue assembled piece to card front.

Ink leaf stamp with yellow and golden yellow inks, using darker color around edges of image; stamp image on rough side of a piece of shrink plastic. Cut out leaf and shrink with heat embossing tool. Let piece cool. Clean stamp and repeat, except use tan and dark brown inks instead of yellow and golden yellow.

Use adhesive dots to attach shrink plastic leaves to ivory card stock; trim an uneven shape around leaves. Ink edges with brown ink. Use double-sided tape to attach assembled piece to top of layered ribbons on card.

For envelope, cut a 7¼ x 5¼-inch piece of gold leaves printed paper; ink edges with brown ink. Glue to front of envelope. Center and glue a 5¼-inch length of multicolored ribbon to a ¾ x 5¼-inch piece of orange card stock; glue layered piece to a 1⅛ x 5¼-inch piece of brown card stock. Glue assembled piece to left side of envelope.

Cut an uneven shape from ivory card stock; ink edges with brown ink. Center and glue to envelope. ■

SOURCES: Printed paper from Creative Imaginations; rubber stamp from Duncan.

Walking through the autumn leaves
Scattered on the ground
Seeing the kaleidoscope
Of colors all around
Listening to the trees' song
As the wind comes rustling through...
May autumn's lovely magic
Bring happiness to you.
    -Unknown

Fall Harvest

Design by JEANNE WYNHOFF

Cut an 8½ x 5½-inch piece of dark brown card stock; score and fold in half. Cut a 4 x 5¼-inch piece of printed paper; ink edges. Cut two 4½-inch lengths of ribbon; wrap both pieces across bottom portion of printed paper, allowing ¼ inch between pieces. Wrap and attach ends to reverse side of printed paper with adhesive dots. Center and attach printed paper to card front with adhesive dots.

Cut off approximately 1½ inches from bottom edge of fabric tag; pull loose fabric strands to fray edge a bit. Loop fibers through hole in tag; set eyelet at top of tag. Run fabric tag through adhesive applicator; attach tag to right side of card at a slight angle.

Using punch, punch four postage stamps from cork sheet; color punched stamps with leafing pen. Ink edges of cork label; set aside to dry.

Cut a strip of printed paper and run it through adhesive applicator; using alphabet dies, die-cut "FALL" from printed paper.

Use adhesive dots to attach cork postage stamps to left side of fabric tag on card, alternating angles of stamps. Attach punched letters to cork postage stamps to spell "FALL." Attach pumpkin and leaf stickers to right side of tag. Use a mini adhesive dot to attach a leaf button to bottom edge of tag.

Attach pumpkin sticker to cork label; use a mini adhesive dot to attach leaf button to lower right corner of cork label. Attach label to lower left corner of card on top of ribbons.

For envelope, use template to trace and cut an envelope from printed paper. Score and fold envelope flaps; glue side and bottom flaps together. Ink edges.

Cut a 1¼ x 1⅜-inch piece of fabric from remaining fabric tag; ink edges and attach to lower right corner of envelope with adhesive dots. Attach pumpkin and leaf stickers to fabric rectangle; attach "FALL" sticker on top of pumpkin sticker. ∎

SOURCES: Printed paper from Frances Meyer Inc.; fabric tags from Fibers By The Yard; ink pad from Clearsnap Inc.; dies and die-cutting tool from Sizzix/Ellison; cork sheet and label from LazerLetterz; punch from EK Success; stickers from Karen Foster Design; leafing pen from Krylon; adhesive applicator and cartridges from Xyron.

MATERIALS

Card stock: dark brown
Printed paper: orange pumpkin print
Stickers: pumpkins, leaves, "FALL"
2 brown fabric tags
Cork sheet
Cork label
Copper leafing pen
Brown eyelet with eyelet setting tool
2 mini leaf buttons
Assorted brown and gray fibers
Brown chalk ink pad
7/16-inch-wide sheer brown with white polka-dots ribbon
Die-cutting tool with alphabet dies
Postage stamp punch
Envelope template to fit a 4¼ x 5½-inch card
Adhesive applicator with permanent adhesive cartridges
Adhesive dots: regular and mini

THERE IS NO SEASON fall

SUCH DELIGHT CAN BRING,

autumn

Autumn Delight DIAGRAMS ON PAGE 153

Design by BARBARA GREVE

Condition air-dry modeling compound by kneading it with hands until it is warm and pliable. On work surface, roll out compound to ⅛-inch thickness. Using alphabet stamps, stamp "FALL" into compound. ***Note:*** *Apply a small amount of watermark ink to each stamp before stamping letter into compound.* Using craft knife, cut a square around each letter; set squares aside to dry.

Cut two 2¾ x 7¾-inch rectangles each from sage green and deep orange card stock. Place one orange and one sage green rectangle next to each other, lining up long edges, with the orange rectangle on the left. Referring to Fig. 1 on page 153, cut out a 3½-inch square window from center of rectangles. Place the remaining rectangles together in the same manner, except place sage green rectangle on left. Referring to Fig. 2 on page 153, cut a 4-inch square window from center; tear bottom edge off opening.

Center and cut a 3½-inch square window from card front, 1 inch from top edge. Adhere first set of rectangles to card front, lining up window with card window. Referring to photo, adhere second set of rectangles to card. Trim edges evenly with card.

To color the "F" modeling compound square, mix equal amounts of gel stain medium and rose pink paint together; paint letter with mixture and wipe off excess with a paper towel. In same manner, use gel stain medium and burgundy paint to add shading to the square.

Continuing in same manner, paint "A" with pale yellow and shade with golden yellow. Paint one "L" with yellow and shade with light brown; paint remaining "L" with orange and shade with dark orange. Let all pieces dry. Lightly sand letters; antique each with deep brown and let dry.

Glue a 5½ x 7¾-inch piece of printed paper inside card. Trim a rectangle around vellum quote and adhere toward lower right corner on card front with vellum tape.

Using craft knife, make a ¼-inch slit in fold of card 2 inches from bottom edge; thread ribbon through slit. Slide round buckle and thread "fall" letter slides onto ribbon, positioning letters on top of vellum quote. Knot ends together inside card; trim ends.

Referring to photo, glue clay letters inside window. Using needle and thread, sew leaf button to upper left corner of opening.

For envelope, use black ink to stamp "FALL" along left side on reverse side of envelope. Cut a piece of yellow vellum to cover "F"; adhere inside envelope behind "F" for color. Punch a ³⁄₁₆-inch hole in center of envelope flap and directly below flap; set looped eyelets. Thread ribbon through eyelet loops and tie a bow; knot each ribbon end and trim. ■

SOURCES: Air-dry modeling compound from Creative Paperclay Co.; printed paper from Arctic Frog; vellum quote from Die Cuts With A View; rubber stamps from Technique Tuesday; slide letters from Making Memories; eyelets from Karen Foster Design; gel stain medium from DecoArt; adhesive from Decorator's Solution.

MATERIALS

- Card stock: sage green, deep orange
- Printed paper: sage green fabric
- 5½ x 7¾-inch white card
- 9 x 6-inch clear vellum envelope
- Yellow vellum
- White air-dry modeling compound
- Acrylic paints: rose pink, burgundy, pale yellow, golden yellow, yellow, light brown, orange, dark orange, deep brown
- Clear gel stain medium
- Large alphabet rubber stamps
- Ink pads: watermark, black dye
- Seasonal vellum quote
- Orange leaf button
- Small acrylic round buckle
- Silver slide letters
- ¼-inch-wide sheer orange ribbon
- Orange all-purpose thread
- 2 silver looped eyelets with eyelet setting tool
- Sandpaper
- Paper towels
- Paintbrush
- Sewing needle
- Craft knife
- Acrylic clay roller *or* brayer
- Vellum tape
- Paper adhesive

MATERIALS

- Card stock: deep red, light green, light tan
- White envelope to fit a 7 x 5-inch card
- Papermaking kit
- Mica dust
- Angel wings: yellow, orange
- Air-dry modeling compound
- Maple leaf rubber stamp
- Ink pads: watermark, black, metallic gold
- Metallic rub-on creams: copper, red, green, yellow
- Black acrylic paint
- Rub-on transfers: "Autumn," assorted autumn-theme sentiments
- Waxed paper
- Acrylic clay roller *or* brayer
- Paintbrush
- Blender
- Sewing machine with gold all-purpose thread
- Craft knife
- Paper adhesive

Maple Leaf

Design by MARY AYRES

Project note: Remove hard brown pods from angel wings before blending pulp.

Following manufacturer's instructions included with papermaking kit, make handmade paper. For green paper, place torn pieces of light green card stock, ¼ teaspoon mica dust and several yellow angel wings in blender and mix. For tan paper, place torn pieces of light tan card stock, ¼ teaspoon mica dust and several orange angel wings in blender and mix. When finished, place sheets of handmade paper between sheets of waxed paper; iron dry.

For card, cut a 7 x 10-inch piece of deep red card stock; score and fold in half. Ink card edges with black and metallic gold inks.

Tear a 6¼ x 4½-inch rectangle from green handmade paper; ink edges with black and gold metallic inks. Center and glue rectangle to card front. Machine-stitch around edges of green rectangle.

Using a craft knife, cut a 2⅜-inch square opening from upper left corner of green rectangle, making sure to not cut sewn edge. In same manner, cut a 4¼ x ¾-inch rectangle opening from lower right corner of green rectangle. Ink opening edges with metallic gold ink.

Transfer "Autumn" to right side of green rectangle. Transfer an autumn sentiment inside card, positioning it so it shows through bottom right opening. Tear a 2¼-inch square from tan handmade paper; glue inside card, positioning square so it shows through upper left opening.

Roll out modeling compound to ⅛-inch thickness on waxed paper. Rub a small amount of watermark ink on leaf stamp; stamp leaf in compound. Let dry. Remove waxed paper from reverse side of leaf; cut out leaf with scissors.

Paint leaf black; let dry. Rub metallic rub-on creams to top surface of leaf. Glue leaf to tan square in upper left opening.

For envelope, cut 1-inch-wide strips from tan and green handmade papers. Tear one long edge off each strip. Overlap and adhere strips to left side of envelope with torn sides facing the same direction. Trim edges evenly with envelope. Transfer an autumn-theme sentiment to green strip. ■

SOURCES: Papermaking kit, mica dust and angel wings from Arnold Grummer's; air-dry modeling compound from Creative Paperclay Co.; rubber stamp from Delta/Rubber Stampede; metallic rub-on creams from Craf-T Products; rub-on transfers from Royal & Langnickel; paper adhesive from Decorator's Solution.

Leaf Montage

Design by SHARON REINHART

Cut an 8½ x 5½-inch piece of metallic brown card stock; score and fold in half. Open card and place front side face down on cutting surface. Using cutting tool and oval template, cut an oval from card front.

Stamp parsley leaf in upper left and lower right corners on front of card; sprinkle both with gold embossing powder and emboss.

Cut a 4 x 5½-inch piece of botanical printed paper. *Note: Cut an area of paper that includes some leaves.* Adhere piece to reverse side of card front, covering oval opening.

Cut two leaves from embossed botanical paper; brush one coat of gloss medium on leaves. Let dry. Using adhesive foam tape and referring to photo, attach embossed leaves to card.

Cut a 4⅛ x 5⅜-inch rectangle from metallic brown card stock; glue to reverse side of card front.

Rub each silk leaf with used fabric softener sheet to reduce static; stamp each leaf with "Thanks" image. Sprinkle leaves with gold embossing powder and emboss. *Note: A wooden skewer is helpful to hold leaves while embossing.* Glue two leaves to lower left corner of card; attach remaining leaf with adhesive foam tape.

For envelope, stamp one parsley leaf to left side of envelope; stamp another parsley leaf to bottom edge. Sprinkle both with gold embossing powder and emboss. ■

SOURCES: Printed papers from K&Company; cutting tool and oval template from Fiskars; rubber stamp from Hero Arts and Fred B. Mullett; gloss medium from Ranger.

MATERIALS

Metallic brown card stock
Printed papers: botanical
   print, embossed
   botanical print
Ivory envelope to fit a
   4⅛ x 5½-inch card
Used fabric softener sheet
Wooden skewer (optional)
3 nonmatching silk leaves
Rubber stamps: "Thanks,"
   parsley leaf
Embossing ink pad
Gold embossing powder
Embossing heat tool
Cutting tool with medium
   oval template
Paintbrush
Clear dimensional gloss
   medium
Paper adhesive
Adhesive foam tape

Leaf Collage

Design by BARBARA GREVE

MATERIALS

5¾ x 7½-inch white card
9 x 6-inch ivory vellum
    envelope
White tissue paper
Fusible web
Pressing paper
Used dryer sheet
Dark pink fibers
Air-dry modeling compound
Maple leaf rubber stamp
Ink pads: embossing,
    brown, green, black
Gold embossing powder
Acrylic paints: red, deep
    red, deep brown
Light green chalk
Copper metallic
    rub-on cream
Sheer antiquing varnish
Spray sealer
¾-inch gold pin back
Iron
Acrylic clay roller *or* brayer
Spray water bottle
Embossing heat tool
Paintbrush
Craft knife
Permanent fabric adhesive
Metal adhesive

Lay the used dryer sheet on top of the shiny side of the pressing paper; lay fusible web on top of dryer sheet. Crumple up tissue paper; smooth it out and lay it on top of the fusible web. Following the manufacturer's instructions on the fusible web, iron the layered pieces together.

Using brown, green and black inks, stamp leaf image randomly on top surface of layered tissue paper. Using embossing ink, stamp two additional leaves on layered tissue paper; emboss leaves with gold embossing powder and let dry.

Condition air-dry modeling compound by kneading it with hands until it is warm and pliable. Roll out compound to ⅛-inch thickness; apply embossing ink to leaf stamp and stamp on compound. Emboss leaf with gold embossing powder. Cut out leaf with craft knife; set aside to dry.

Add water to a small amount of deep brown paint; apply small amounts of thinned paint randomly to layered tissue paper. Let dry. Spread a layer of antiquing varnish on tissue paper; let dry. Tear layered tissue paper to 5 x 7 inches. Set scraps aside.

Mix a small amount of deep brown paint with red paint; dip the edges of the layered tissue paper in the mixture. Spray a mist of water on edges to allow colors to run slightly; use heat tool to dry edges.

Tear a 3-inch square from leftover layered tissue paper; dip edges in same mixture as above; dry edges with heat tool.

Rub light green chalk on edges of modeling compound leaf; rub metallic cream on leaf. Spray top surface of leaf with sealer; let dry. Use metal adhesive to glue pin back to reverse side of leaf; let dry.

Using fabric adhesive, center and glue large piece of tissue paper to card. Tie fibers around leaf pin stem; lay small piece of layered tissue paper in upper left corner of card. Pin leaf pin through tissue paper and card to secure.

For envelope, use embossing ink to stamp a leaf overlapping envelope flap; emboss with gold embossing powder and let dry. ∎

SOURCES: Air-dry modeling compound from Creative Paperclay Co.; rubber stamp and varnish from Delta/Rubber Stampede; metallic rub-on cream from Craf-T Products; Glass, Metal & More and Fabri-Tac adhesives from Beacon.

Autumn Mosaic

Design by BARBARA GREVE

MATERIALS

5⅛ x 7-inch yellow card
    and envelope
Printed papers: autumn
    leaf, brown gingham,
    black gingham
Yellow vellum
Orange acrylic round buckle
Orange round leaf charm
Ribbons: ⁷⁄₁₆-inch-wide
    yellow/orange
    gingham, ¼-inch-wide
    sheer orange
Small leaf punch
Craft knife
Stapler with staples
Paper adhesive
Vellum tape
Computer font (optional)

Cut a 4⅝ x 6½-inch piece of autumn leaf paper; center and glue to card. Referring to photo, use craft knife to cut a 3⅛ x 2⅜-inch window from card front.

Using craft knife, make a ½-inch slit in fold of card 2¼ inches from bottom edge; thread gingham ribbon through slit. Slide buckle on ribbon, positioning buckle centered below window. With ribbon ends inside card, trim ends and adhere. Apply glue to buckle to secure.

Thread sheer ribbon through leaf charm; staple ribbon to upper right corner of card. Trim ribbon ends.

Cut a 5 x 7-inch piece of black gingham paper; adhere inside card. Trim edges evenly with card. Use a computer to generate, or hand-print, desired autumn-theme sentiment on vellum; trim a 2¾ x 2⅛-inch rectangle around sentiment. Use vellum tape to attach sentiment to brown gingham paper; trim edges evenly. Center and glue layered piece inside card window.

For envelope, punch out several leaves along edge of envelope flap. Cut a strip of autumn leaf paper and adhere underneath flap so printed paper shows through punched leaves. ∎

SOURCES: Printed papers from Hot Off The Press, Bo-Bunny Press and K&Company; charm and buckle from Junkitz; adhesive from Decorator's Solution.

Trick or Treat Trio DIAGRAM ON PAGE 154

Designs by SUSAN HUBER

Cut a 4 x 8-inch piece of black card stock; score and fold in half. Determine if a top fold or side fold card is desired. Cut a piece of orange card stock slightly smaller than card front; tear off bottom edge if desired. Wrap fibers around card stock as desired and secure with a knot or candy corn brad.

For ghost and jack-o'-lantern cards, die cut images from orange or white card stock. Using foam tape, adhere images to black card stock; cut a rectangle around images to fit on orange card stock. Adhere assembled panels to card fronts. Embellish with buttons or black brads.

For candy corn card, use embossing stylus and brass stencil to emboss each section of candy corn to white, yellow and orange card stock. Cut out each piece, leaving a ⅛-inch border. Referring to photo, adhere pieces together, forming a candy corn. Draw face on candy corn; adhere piece to black card stock with foam tape. Cut a rectangle around candy corn; punch a ¹⁄₁₆-inch hole through each corner and insert orange brads. Glue assembled panel to card front.

For envelopes, use provided pattern to trace and draw an envelope from black card stock; score and fold on dashed lines to form envelope flaps. Glue side and bottom flaps together. Attach desired stickers to envelope. ∎

SOURCES: Die-cutting tool and dies from QuicKutz Inc.; stickers from Karen Foster Design; candy corn brad from Queen & Co.; stencil from Lasting Impressions for Paper Inc.

MATERIALS

Card stock: black, orange, white
Dies: jack-o'-lantern, ghost
Stickers: Halloween-theme
Brass stencil: candy corn
Fibers: black, white, yellow, orange
Black fine-tip marker
Buttons: 4 orange mini round
Mini round brads: 4 orange, 2 black
Candy corn brad
¼-inch-wide black gingham ribbon
Die-cutting tool
Embossing stylus
¹⁄₁₆-inch hole punch
Foam tape
Glue stick

Spooky Spiderwebs

Design by SANDRA GRAHAM SMITH

MATERIALS

- Card stock: orange, black
- Rubber stamps: "trick or treat!," spiderweb
- Black dye ink pad
- Spider embellishment
- Envelope to fit a 9 x 4-inch card
- Stamp positioner (optional)
- Glue stick
- Tacky glue

Cut a 9 x 7¾-inch piece of orange card stock; score and fold in half. Stamp spiderwebs on card front in a wavy pattern, referring to photo for placement. *Option: Use a stamp positioner to ensure spiderwebs are positioned next to each other.* Cut along bottom edges of spider webs.

Cut a 9 x 3⅞-inch piece of black card stock; use glue stick to adhere inside card so it shows at bottom of card front.

Stamp "trick or treat!" on orange card stock; cut a rectangle around sentiment. Use glue stick to glue rectangle to black card stock; trim a small border. Glue to upper right corner of card front.

Use tacky glue to glue spider embellishment to right side of card on spiderwebs.

For envelope, carefully take apart premade envelope and use as a template to trace and cut an envelope from orange card stock; score and fold to form envelope flaps. Glue side and bottom flaps together. Stamp spiderwebs on lower left corner of envelope front and on center of top envelope flap.

SOURCES: Rubber stamps from The Rubbernecker Stamp Co. and Duncan.

Bunch of Bats DIAGRAM ON PAGE 153

Design by KATHLEEN PANEITZ

Cut a 5½ x 8¾-inch piece of white card stock; score and fold in half. Cut a 5½ x 4⅜-inch piece of black card stock; glue to card front.

Cut a 5⅜ x 4⅛-inch piece of Halloween-theme text printed paper; ink edges. Wrap ribbon around bottom portion of paper, securing ribbon with double-sided tape. Tie a knot on front and trim ends.

Using circle cutter, cut a 3⅜-inch-diameter circle from yellow card stock; ink edges and surface. Glue circle to upper left corner of paper; trim top edge even. Punch four ¹⁄₁₆-inch holes randomly through paper; set bat eyelets. Glue assembled panel to card.

Stamp "Trick or Treat" on yellow moon on card. Cut eight ⅛-inch-wide strips of black card stock. Using quilling tool and referring to provided patterns, quill one strip into a circle; quill one strip into a bat body and the six remaining strips into marquise shapes, varying them in size. Use mini adhesive dots to secure ends on quilled shapes. Referring to photo for placement, glue quilled shapes to card, forming a bat. Glue wiggly eyes to bat.

For envelope, use template to trace and cut an envelope from white paper; score and fold to form envelope flaps. Glue side and bottom flaps together. Ink edges and drag black ink pad across surface several times. Stamp "Trick or Treat" in lower left corner of envelope front. Using template again, cut a piece of metallic silver paper to fit inside top envelope flap; slip paper inside envelope and glue. ∎

SOURCES: Printed paper from Daisy D's Paper Co.; rubber stamp from Duncan; eyelets from The Stamp Doctor; template from The C-Thru Ruler Co.

MATERIALS

Card stock: black, white, yellow
Printed paper: Halloween-theme text
White paper
Metallic silver paper
Rubber stamp: "Trick or Treat"
Black dye ink pad
Small set of wiggly eyes
⅝-inch-wide black gingham wire-edge ribbon
4 bat eyelets with eyelet-setting tool
Envelope template to fit a 5½ x 4⅜-inch card
¹⁄₁₆-inch hole punch
Quilling tool
Circle cutter
Mini adhesive dots
Double-sided tape
Paper adhesive

Halloween Crosswords

Design by SUSAN STRINGFELLOW

MATERIALS

Card stock: orange, yellow, olive green

Coordinating printed papers: black/orange striped, white with multicolored polka dots

Rubber stamps: small alphabet

Black dye ink pad

"Halloween" charm tile

Black cat button

Mini round brads: 1 lime green, 2 black

Black round eyelets with eyelet-setting tool

⅜-inch-wide orange gingham ribbon

Envelope template to fit a 5-inch square card

Circle punches: ¹⁄₁₆-inch, 1¼-inch, 1½-inch

Sandpaper *or* sanding block

Adhesive foam squares

Paper adhesive

Cut a 10 x 5-inch piece of orange card stock; score and fold in half. Sand card edges. Cut an 1⅜ x 5-inch piece of black/orange striped paper; glue to left side of card. Cut a 3⅜ x 2¾-inch rectangle from polka-dot paper; referring to photo, glue rectangle to upper right portion of card, overlapping right edge of black/orange striped piece.

Stamp several Halloween-theme words inside the polka dots. Punch a ¹⁄₁₆-inch hole through lower right corner of card front. Insert lime green brad through Halloween charm tile and through punched hole to secure tile to card. Stamp "happy" above tile.

Punch a 1½-inch circle from orange card stock and a 1¼-inch circle from yellow card stock; sand the edges of both. Glue the yellow circle to orange circle, slightly off-center. Punch a ¹⁄₁₆-inch hole at top and bottom of layered circles; set eyelets. Glue cat button to circles.

Cut a 5¾-inch length of ribbon; thread ribbon through eyelets, threading both ends from back to front. Place ribbon vertically on left side of card, positioning assembled circle toward top of card. Adhere circle to card with adhesive foam squares to give dimension. Punch a ¹⁄₁₆-inch hole at top and bottom of ribbon; insert black brads. Trim ribbon ends into V-notches.

For envelope, use template to trace and cut an envelope from olive green card stock; score and fold to form envelope flaps. Sand edges. Glue side and bottom flaps together.

Cut a 5⅛ x ⅞-inch piece of polka-dot paper; glue to front of envelope ⅝ inch from bottom edge. Stamp "boo" inside polka dots. ■

SOURCES: Printed papers, charm tile and button from Doodlebug Design Inc.; rubber stamps from Hero Arts; Coluzzle template from Provo Craft.

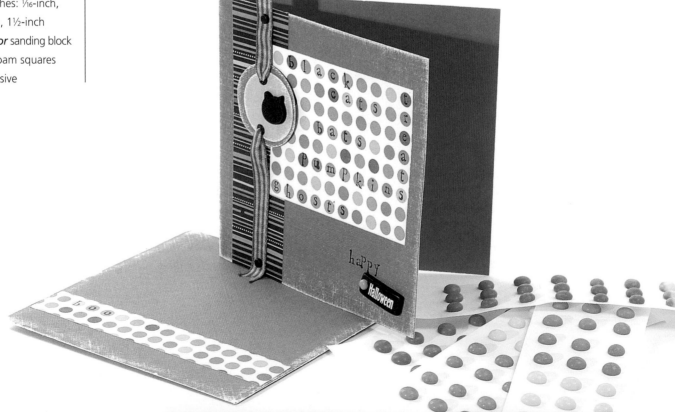

Bewitching

Design by J E A N N E   W Y N H O F F

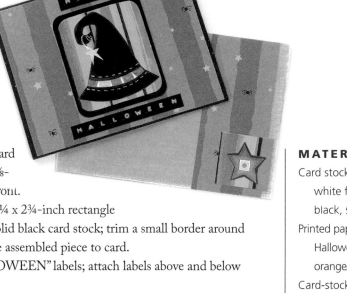

Cut a 5½ x 8½-inch piece of black white-flecked card stock; score and fold in half. Center and glue a 5¼ x 4⅛-inch piece of purple Halloween-theme paper to card front.

Attach witch's hat sticker to striped paper; cut a 2¼ x 2¾-inch rectangle around sticker. Round corners with punch. Glue to solid black card stock; trim a small border around paper and round corners with punch. Center and glue assembled piece to card.

Using label maker, make "HAPPY" and "HALLOWEEN" labels; attach labels above and below witch's hat.

For envelope, use template to trace and cut an envelope from solid orange card stock. Score and fold on lines to form envelope flaps; glue side and bottom flaps together. Sand edges.

Cut a 1⅞ x 4¼-inch piece of purple Halloween-theme paper; glue to right side of envelope front. Attach star sticker to striped paper; cut a 1⅜-inch square around sticker. Glue to lower right corner of envelope. ■

SOURCES: Printed papers from Creative Imaginations and Frances Meyer Inc.; stickers from O' Scrap; template from Duncan.

MATERIALS

Card stock: black with white flecks, solid black, solid orange
Printed papers: purple Halloween-theme, orange/purple striped
Card-stock stickers: witch's hat, star
Sandpaper
Envelope template to fit a 5½ x 4¼-inch card
Label maker with black label tape
Rounded corner punch
Glue stick

A Little Batty

Design by J E A N N E   W Y N H O F F

Cut a 5½ x 8½-inch piece of black card stock; score and fold in half. Cut a 5¼ x 4-inch piece of striped paper; cut a 5¾-inch piece of ribbon. Adhere ribbon across striped paper 1 inch from top edge; wrap and adhere ends to reverse side of paper. Center and adhere assembled panel to card front.

Attach bat sticker to upper left corner of card, overlapping ribbon. Attach "trick or treat" sticker to right side of card; punch one 1/16-inch hole through center of star and three 1/16-inch holes, evenly spaced, along bottom edge of sticker. Insert brads.

For envelope, use template to trace and cut an envelope from black card stock; use template again to trace and cut top envelope flap portion from striped paper, cutting an additional 2 inches along bottom edge. Adhere striped paper to reverse side of black envelope, lining up top edges. Score and fold on lines to form envelope flaps; adhere side and bottom flaps together.

Cut a 1¾ x 4¼-inch piece of striped paper; glue to left side of envelope front. Attach spider stickers to bottom of striped paper. ■

SOURCES: Printed paper from Creative Imaginations; stickers from O' Scrap; template from Duncan.

MATERIALS

Black card stock
Printed paper: orange/purple striped
Card-stock stickers: bat, 2 spiders, "trick or treat" rectangle with star
⅜-inch-wide black grosgrain ribbon
Envelope template to fit a 5½ x 4¼-inch card
4 black round brads
1/16-inch hole punch
Adhesive dots

A Time for Thanks

Design by LINDA BEESON

MATERIALS

Card stock: brown,
    scrap piece of red
Printed papers: 2
    coordinating prints
Brown business-size
    envelope with
    string clasp
Chipboard
Stickers: alphabet
Mini rub-on transfer:
    "a time to give thanks"
3 various ribbons
Jute
Mini tags: 1 plain, 1 "fall"
Ink pads: brown,
    golden yellow
Wooden stir stick
Sandpaper
Punches: small leaf,
    rounded corner,
    ⅝-inch square
Paper adhesive

Cut a 9 x 8-inch piece of brown card stock; score and fold in half, forming a 9 x 4-inch card. Cut four 2 x 3¼-inch rectangles from printed papers, two from each print. Round corners of each with punch. Sand edges. Glue rounded rectangles, evenly spaced, to card front.

Attach alphabet stickers to spell "Thankful" to chipboard. Cut a shape around each letter. Glue letters, evenly spaced, across center of card front.

Transfer "a time to give thanks" to right side of stir stick. Cut a 3-inch length of each ribbon. Fold each ribbon in half and loop each around left end of stir stick; trim ends at an angle.

Rub ink pads across plain mini tag; punch a small leaf from red card stock. Glue leaf to tag. Thread jute through tag and tie into a knot around left end of stir stick. Trim ends. Glue stick and tag to card below letters.

To embellish envelope, punch four ⅝-inch squares from printed papers. Sand edges. Glue across center of top envelope flap. Ink edges of envelope brown. Rub ink pads across "fall" mini tag; ink edges brown. Tie tag onto string clasp. ■

SOURCES: Printed papers from Chatterbox Inc.; stickers, mini tags and rub-on transfers from Making Memories; envelope from Paper Zone.

Bountiful Charms

Design by S U S A N   S T R I N G F E L L O W

Cut an 11 x 5½-inch piece of cream card stock; score and fold in half, forming a 5½-inch square card. Using light brown antique-finish ink, stamp Thanksgiving sentiment randomly to card front; ink card edges with both antique-finish inks. Stamp sentiment inside card if desired.

Cut a 6-inch length of ribbon and a 6-inch length of fiber. Cut right end of ribbon into a V-notch. Place fiber on center of ribbon and machine-stitch them both to card 1¾ inch from top edge, lining up left edges.

Cut a 3³⁄₁₆ x 3¾-inch rectangle from green handmade paper; tear off bottom edge. Center and glue rectangle to card front; machine-stitch top and side edges.

Using black solvent-based ink, stamp three fruit or vegetable images onto shrink plastic; let dry. Lightly sponge entire surface of two stamped images with light brown antique-finish ink. Use dye inks to paint two images; let dry.

Cut out images and punch a hole through center top of each. Use heat embossing tool to shrink pieces or shrink in an oven, following manufacturer's instructions. Attach a jump ring to each image. Set aside.

Using black solvent-based ink, stamp fruit bowl image onto cream card stock; cut a 2⅜-inch square around image, allowing additional space along bottom edge for eyelets. Paint image using dye inks. Sponge edges with antique-finish inks. Glue to burgundy card stock; trim a small border.

Punch four ⅛-inch holes, evenly spaced, along bottom edge of layered image. Set eyelets. Begin to thread wire through eyelets, wrapping and twisting wire as desired and attaching the three fruit or vegetable charms across the bottom, placing white charm in the center. Curl wire ends to secure, using round-nose pliers if needed. Attach assembled piece to center of green rectangle with adhesive foam squares.

For envelope, use template to trace and cut an envelope from cream card stock; score and fold to form envelope flaps. Using light brown antique-finish ink, stamp Thanksgiving sentiment over surface of top envelope flap. Ink edges with antique-finish inks. ∎

SOURCES: Rubber stamps from Stampin' Up!; solvent ink pad from Tsukineko Inc.; antique-finish ink pads from Ranger; wire from Artistic Wire; Coluzzle template from Provo Craft.

MATERIALS

Card stock: cream, burgundy
Green handmade paper
Rubber stamps: Thanksgiving sentiment, bowl of fruit, 3 single fruit or vegetable images
Black solvent-based ink pad
Dye ink pads: olive green, burgundy, golden yellow, purple
Antique-finish ink pads: ivory, light brown
Shrink plastic
24-gauge gunmetal wire
4 brass eyelets with eyelet-setting tool
3 silver jump rings
⅝-inch-wide burgundy grosgrain ribbon
Golden yellow fiber
Envelope template to fit a 5½-inch square card
Craft sponges
Paintbrush
⅛-inch hole punch
Round-nose pliers (optional)
Wire nippers
Sewing machine with light brown all-purpose thread
Embossing heat tool *or* oven
Adhesive foam squares
Paper adhesive

So Thankful

Design by SUSAN STRINGFELLOW

MATERIALS

4¼ x 5½-inch brown
    card with envelope,
    purchased
Printed papers: white with
    brown polka dots,
    ivory with multicolored
    polka dots
Rubber stamps: small
    alphabet
Mini paper bag
2 small paper flowers
Twill tape with printed
    "family" text
Round cork buckle
⅜-inch-wide dusty blue
    grosgrain ribbon
Brown dye ink pad
Sewing machine with
    brown all-purpose
    thread
Permanent paper adhesive
Computer font (optional)

Cut a 4 x 5¼-inch piece of white polka-dot print paper; ink edges and glue to card front. Machine-stitch around edge of white polka-dot paper.

Ink edges of paper bag and use alphabet stamps to stamp "so thankful" in top left corner of bag. Glue bag to left side of card.

Use a computer to generate, or hand-print, several things to be thankful for on ivory polka-dot paper. Cut a rectangle around each sentiment; ink edges and insert them inside paper bag.

Cut a 7 x ⅞-inch piece of ivory polka-dot paper; crumple up paper and then smooth it out. Ink edges. Machine-stitch a 4¼-inch piece of printed twill tape to center of paper. Cut the layered strip diagonally 1½ inch from right edge; glue small piece ¾ inch from bottom edge of card, lining up right edges. Thread longer piece through cork buckle, positioning buckle toward right end; adhere piece ¾ inch from bottom edge, lining up left edges, forming the appearance of a belt.

Cut a 2-inch length of ribbon; tie a knot in center. Place two paper flowers just above cork buckle, adhering ribbon knot over flower stems to secure them in place.

For envelope, cut a 5¾ x 2-inch piece of white polka-dot paper; ink edges and glue across center of envelope front. Cut a ½ x 4⅜-inch piece of ivory polka-dot paper; ink edges and glue to left side of envelope. Cut a 2-inch length of ribbon; tie a knot in center. Glue knot to center edge of ivory strip. ∎

SOURCES: Printed papers from SEI; twill from 7 gypsies; rubber stamps from Hero Arts; bag and flowers from Self-Addressed; cork buckle from LazerLetterz.

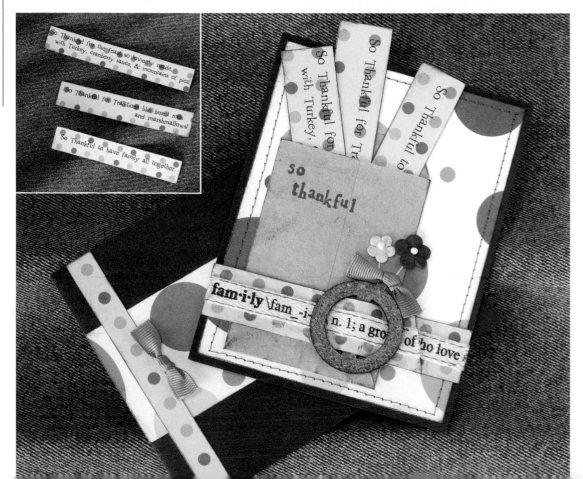

Thankful for You

Design by J U L I E   R Y V E R

Cut a 6 x 12-inch piece of brown card stock; score and fold in half. Tear a 5½-inch square from burgundy crackle print paper; ink edges and glue to card front.

Using adhesive dots, adhere two silk leaves to center of card front, overlapping each other. Wrap ribbon around bottom portion of card front and tie a knot on front; trim ends. Use adhesive dots to secure ribbon.

Use a computer to generate, or hand-print, "Give Thanks" on tan card stock; cut a rectangle around words to fit on accent bar. Ink edges of rectangle. Glue rectangle to accent bar; attach bar to card, overlapping edges of leaves.

For envelope, glue a sheet of burgundy and brown crackle print papers together, white sides facing each other. Lay paper on work surface, burgundy side face down; use template to trace and cut an envelope from paper. Score and fold to form envelope flaps. Ink edges.

Tear a 1⅞-inch square from brown crackle print paper; ink edges and glue square to what will be the lower right corner on reverse side of envelope. Place a silk leaf on top of square and punch a ¹⁄₁₆-inch hole through lower edge of leaf and square; insert brad. Glue side and bottom flaps together. ■

SOURCES: Printed papers from Colorbök and K&Company; accent bar from All My Memories; template from Green Sneakers Inc.

MATERIALS

Card stock: brown, tan
Printed papers: burgundy crackle, brown crackle
Bronze accent bar
⁹⁄₁₆-inch-wide brown satin ribbon
Silk autumn-colored leaves
Bronze mini square brad
Brown dye ink pad
Envelope template to fit a 6-inch square card
¹⁄₁₆-inch hole punch
Glue stick
Adhesive dots
Computer font (optional)

Holiday Assortment DIAGRAMS ON PAGE 155

Designs by HEATHER D. WHITE

MATERIALS

Card stock: white

Printed papers: red/green striped, green circle print

2 white envelopes to fit 4¼ x 5½-inch cards

Stickers: assorted Christmas-theme sentiments, Christmas presents, Christmas trees, stars, holly berries with leaves, Rudolph with red nose, mittens

Brown dye ink pad

Red twine

6 silver eyelet brads

Christmas-theme family photo

Double-sided tape

Glue stick

Paper adhesive

Project note: Lightly ink the edges and surfaces of all stickers and papers before attaching to card.

FROM OUR FAMILY TO YOURS

Cut a 6 x 8½-inch piece of white card stock; score and fold in half. Ink edges of card. Attach a Christmas-theme sentiment sticker to bottom edge of card. Cut a 1 x 3½-inch rectangle from striped paper; glue to right side of card.

Attach another Christmas-theme sentiment next to striped rectangle. Attach Christmas tree and star stickers to striped rectangle on right side of card.

Trim family photo to 3¹¹⁄₁₆ x 3⁷⁄₁₆ inches; use double-sided tape to attach photo to empty area on card front.

For envelope, cut a 6¾ x 10¾-inch piece of white card stock. Referring to Fig. 1 on page 155, score and fold dashed lines, forming an envelope. Secure sides of envelope shut with double-sided tape. Trim sides of top envelope flap at an angle; lightly ink edges.

Cut two pieces from striped paper, one measuring 6¾ x 1 inch and the other 6¾ x ⁹⁄₁₆ inch. Glue small piece to top edge of envelope front; glue remaining piece to bottom edge of envelope front. Attach a Christmas present and a Christmas-theme sentiment sticker to envelope front, leaving empty space in center.

TIS ... THE SEASON

Cut a 5½ x 8½-inch piece of white card stock; score and fold in half. Ink edges and surface of card front. Cut a 5¼ x 4-inch rectangle from striped paper; center and glue to card front.

Cut a 2½ x 4¼-inch piece of green circle print paper; tear off long edges. Glue to card approximately 1 inch from left edge.

Attach Christmas tree and star stickers to torn strip on card. Attach a Christmas-theme sentiment sticker to right side of card front. Insert three eyelet brads below Christmas sentiment sticker.

For envelope, ink edges of a white envelope. Cut a 2 x 4¼-inch piece of striped paper; glue to left side of envelope front. Cut a 1¾ x 4¼-inch piece of green circle print paper; tear off long edges. Glue to left side of envelope, on top of striped piece. Attach Rudolph sticker to lower left corner of envelope.

YOU MAKE ME MERRY

Cut an 8½ x 5½-inch piece of white card stock; score and fold in half. Ink edges and reverse side of card. Cut a 4¼ x 5½-inch piece of green circle print paper; glue to card.

Cut four 4¼ x ¾-inch strips from striped paper; referring to photo, glue to card, evenly spaced. Attach Christmas-theme sentiment and holly berries with leaves stickers to card. Insert three eyelet brads in upper left corner on top striped strip.

For envelope, ink edges of a white envelope. Cut an 1¹⁄₁₆ x 4⅜-inch rectangle from striped paper; glue to left side of envelope front. Attach Christmas-theme sentiment and Christmas present stickers to envelope front.

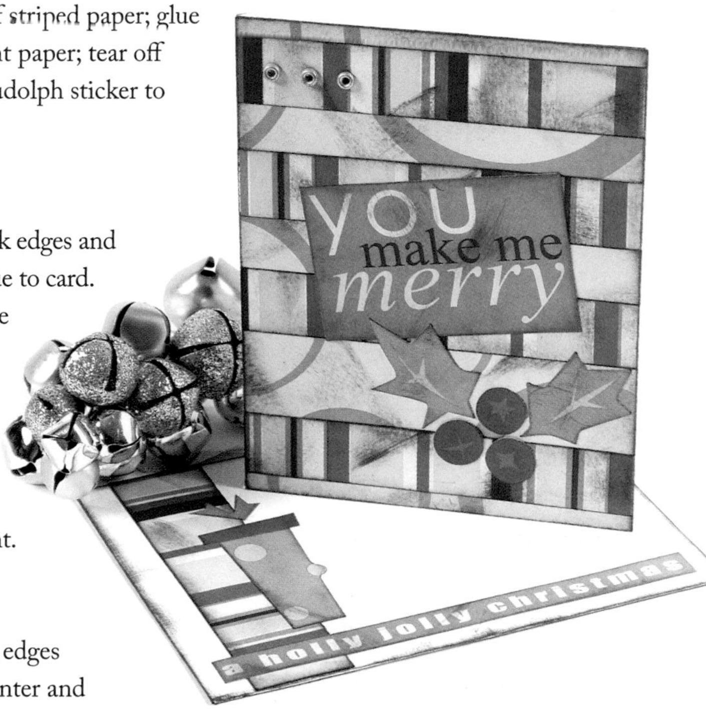

SEASON OF LOVE

Cut a 3½ x 7-inch piece of white card stock; score and fold in half. Ink edges and surface of card. Cut a 3¼-inch square from green circle print paper; center and glue to card.

Cut a 3½ x 1-inch piece of striped paper; attach to card front ⅞ inch from top edge. Attach a Christmas-theme sentiment sticker to lower right corner of card.

Attach mitten stickers to card, leaving tops of mittens unattached. Tie red twine around tops of mittens, connecting mittens. Attach tops of mittens to card. Slightly twist red twine; glue twine to card with paper adhesive.

For envelope, cut a 4 x 10¼-inch rectangle from white card stock; referring to Fig. 2 on page 155, score and fold dashed lines, forming an envelope. Ink edges. Secure sides shut with double-sided tape. Trim sides of top envelope flap at an angle. Ink edges.

Cut a 3¼ x 2-inch rectangle from green circle print paper; cut a 3⅛ x 1⅛-inch rectangle from striped paper. Glue green circle print rectangle to bottom edge of envelope; glue striped piece to right side, overlapping green rectangle. Attach a Christmas-theme sentiment sticker to striped rectangle. ■

SOURCE: Printed papers, stickers, eyelet brads and twine from Pebbles Inc.

MATERIALS

Dark green and white
   card stock
Christmas-themed red and
   green patterned paper
Santa hat rubber stamp
Black ink pad
Iridescent glitter flakes
¼-inch-wide red
   gingham ribbon
Red fine-tip marker
White "Twas the night
   before" rub-on transfer
Envelope template to fit a
   6½ x 4-inch card
White embroidery floss
4 white buttons
Sewing needle
Clear dimensional adhesive
⅛-inch-wide double-sided
   tape

Almost Ready for Christmas

Design by KATHLEEN PANEITZ

Score and fold a 6½ x 8-inch piece of dark green card stock in half, forming a 6½ x 4-inch card. Stamp Santa hat onto white card stock; color with red marker. Apply a layer of clear dimensional adhesive to Santa hat trim and ball at end of hat; sprinkle glitter flakes onto adhesive. Let dry and tap off excess glitter flakes. Trim a 2½ x 2¼-inch rectangle around image. Glue on right side of card.

Cut four pieces of ribbon to fit around edges of white rectangle; adhere as a border with double-sided tape.

Position a button in one corner of rectangle; thread sewing needle with white embroidery floss and sew button onto card. Tie floss into a knot and trim ends. Repeat for remaining three corners. Transfer "Twas the night before" on left side of card.

For envelope, use envelope template to trace and cut an envelope from patterned paper. Score and fold envelope flaps; adhere side and bottom flaps together. ■

SOURCES: Rubber stamp and Aleene's Paper Glaze from Duncan; glitter flakes from Magic Scraps; patterned paper from Autumn Leaves; rub-on transfer from Making Memories; envelope template from The C-Thru Ruler Co.

Pat's Sled

Design by CHRIS NIEMEIER

Score and fold a 6 x 11-inch piece of dark green card stock in half, forming a 6 x 5½-inch card. Cut a 5 x 4-inch rectangle of white card stock; apply bluish-gray chalk to top portion of rectangle. Referring to photo, use gray ink to stamp bare trees along chalked area. Continue stamping trees several times as ink fades to create the appearance of trees in the distance.

Referring to photo for placement, use black ink to stamp the young girl and sled images onto the white rectangle. Use olive green ink to stamp a small fir tree on top of sled horizontally as if the young girl is pulling the tree with her sled.

Color stamped images; add snow prints and sled tracks with light blue pencil. Use black marker to draw lines from the girl's hand to the sled to form a handle. Apply clear glitter glue to girl's coat and hat trim; add tiny dots of clear glitter glue randomly across entire rectangle.

Layer image onto metallic gold card stock; trim a small border. Center and adhere to card. ■

SOURCES: Rubber stamps from Inkadinkado and Coronado Island Designs & Stamps; watermark ink pad from Tsukineko Inc.

MATERIALS

Card stock: dark green, white and metallic gold
Rubber stamps: young girl in winter coat, small fir tree, bare trees, sled and snowflake
Colored pencils
Bluish-gray chalk
Clear glitter glue
Ink pads: gray, black, olive green and watermark
Black fine-tip marker
Glue stick

MATERIALS

Card stock: white, ivory
   and ivory textured
White pearlescent
   snowflake embossed
   vellum
Ivory tag
Twill tape
3 quilled snowflake stickers
Silver snowflake sticker
Black ink pad
Black alphabet rub-on
   transfers
Envelope template to fit a
   5⅞ x 3¾-inch card
Paper glue
Double-sided tape
Computer font (optional)

Delicate Snowflakes

Design by KATHLEEN PANEITZ

Cut a 5⅞ x 7½-inch piece of white card stock; score and fold in half. Glue a 5⅞ x 3¾-inch piece of ivory textured card stock to card front. Cut a 5⅜ x 3-inch rectangle from embossed vellum; tear off bottom edge and attach to card.

Use a computer or hand-print "dreaming of a white" onto tag; rub black ink on edges of tag. Thread twill tape through hole in tag and tie into a bow. Trim ends of twill tape diagonally. Center and attach onto embossed vellum.

Transfer "Christmas…" along bottom edge of card. Attach quilled snowflake stickers to card as desired.

Use envelope template to trace and cut an envelope from ivory card stock; score and fold envelope flaps. Glue side and bottom flaps together. Attach silver snowflake sticker in lower left corner of envelope. ∎

SOURCES: Embossed vellum from Paper Adventures; stickers from EK Success; rub-on transfers from Making Memories; envelope template from The C-Thru Ruler Co.

Winter Panorama

Design by CHRIS NIEMEIER

Score and fold a 10 x 7-inch piece of navy card stock in half, forming a 5 x 7-inch card. Use watermark ink to stamp snowflakes randomly onto the top portion of card front; emboss snowflakes with clear glitter embossing powder.

Cut a 3⅝ x 4½-inch piece of white card stock; tear off bottom edge. Use dark blue ink to stamp winter scene toward center top of torn card stock; stamp "Merry Christmas" below image with same ink. Use blender pen to create snow shadows on winter scene by carefully pulling ink away from image.

Glue stamped card stock to silver card stock; trim a small border around white panel with image. Center and glue layered rectangle onto card. Add tiny dots onto stamped white card stock with clear glitter glue; let dry.

For inside card, cut a 9¾ x 6¾-inch piece of light blue paper; score and fold in half. Glue paper inside card. Stamp Christmas sentiment inside with dark blue ink.

To embellish envelope, lay a torn piece of white paper on top of envelope, allowing a small portion of left side exposed. Use stipple brush and dark blue ink to add color to exposed area. With torn paper still on envelope, stamp snowflakes in exposed area with dark blue ink. Use silver ink to stamp small splatters over entire envelope front. ∎

SOURCES: Rubber stamps from Paper Inspirations Inc. and DeNami Design.

MATERIALS

Card stock: navy, white and silver metallic

Ink pads: silver metallic, dark blue and watermark

Rubber stamps: winter scene, "Merry Christmas", Christmas sentiment, snowflake and small splatter

White and light blue paper

White envelope to fit a 5 x 7-inch card

Blender pen

Clear glitter glue

Clear glitter embossing powder

Embossing heat tool

Stipple brush

Glue stick

MATERIALS

Card stock: red, green,
   black, white and cream
Round Santa Claus and
   holly border
   rubber stamp
Black ink pad
Markers
Colored pencils
Peach and pink chalk
Transparency sheet
Silver washer eyelets
"'tis the season" printed
   red ribbon
"Believe" rub-on transfer
Red rhinestones
Envelope template to fit
   a 4¾-inch diameter
   round card
Holly border punch
³⁄₁₆-inch hole punch
Circle cutter
Mini adhesive dots
Glue stick
Craft glue

'Tis the Season

Design by KATHLEEN PANEITZ

Project note: *Use circle cutter to cut all circles in project.*

Stamp Santa Claus image onto white card stock; cut a 3⅛-inch-diameter circle around image. Color image with markers, colored pencils and chalk.

Cut a 3⅜-inch-diameter circle from black card stock, a 4³⁄₁₆-inch-diameter circle from red card stock, two 4¾-inch-diameter circles from green card stock and one 4¾-inch-diameter circle from transparency.

Layer and adhere all circles together, except for one green circle and transparency circle. Place transparency circle on top of layered circles and place remaining green circle behind layered circles; punch two ³⁄₁₆-inch holes on left side of circles. With transparency circle and first green circle together, attach washer eyelets through holes. Attach washer eyelets through holes of remaining green circle.

Stack circles together and thread printed ribbon through eyelets; tie into a knot and trim ends. Punch four holly leaves from green card stock; outline leaves with green marker. Referring to photo, adhere to transparency.

Use mini adhesive dots to attach red rhinestones as holly berries. Transfer "Believe" onto transparency.

Use envelope template to trace and cut an envelope from red card stock. ***Note:*** *Template measurements may need to be adjusted slightly to fit card.* Score and fold envelope flaps; adhere side and bottom flaps together.

Stamp holly border image onto cream card stock; color with markers. Cut a strip of stamped border the height of the envelope; outline edges with a light green marker. Adhere along left side of envelope. ■

SOURCES: Rubber stamps and border punch from Plaid/All Night Media; washer eyelets from Creative Impressions; ribbon and rub-on transfer from Making Memories; envelope template from The C-Thru Ruler Co.

Recipes for Christmas DIAGRAMS ON PAGES 155 AND 156

Design by MARY AYRES

Cut a 10 x 8-inch rectangle from white card stock; score and fold in half. Use pattern provided to trace and cut a large jar shape from card. **Note:** *Do not cut straight left edge of jar*

Use same pattern to cut the jar lid from desired patterned paper; trim bottom edge with pinking shears. Rub edges with gold ink. Glue lid to card, trimming edges as needed. Rub bottom and side edges of jar with gold ink.

For jar label, attach a tag sticker to patterned paper; tear a rectangle around sticker and rub gold ink on edges.

Use a computer font or hand-print desired holiday words onto vellum; tear a 1-inch-wide strip around words. Place strip diagonally across center of jar label; trim ends evenly with label. Rub vellum edges with gold ink. Lay strip on top of jar label and punch ¹⁄₁₆-inch holes at both ends of strip; attach gold brads. Center and glue label to jar.

Wrap gold ribbon around jar lid and tie into a bow; trim ends into V-notches.

To make small jar card, follow same instructions as for large jar, but cut an 8½ x 5½-inch rectangle from beige card stock instead of a large rectangle from white and use small jar pattern instead of large.

To embellish envelopes, rub edges with gold ink. Glue a piece of ribbon along left edge; trim ends evenly. Adhere tag sticker to patterned paper; tear edges. Rub gold ink on edges.

Use a computer font or hand-print desired name onto vellum; tear a ½-inch-wide strip around name. Place vellum across tag; punch a ⅛-inch hole at left side and attach an eyelet.

Thread ribbon through eyelet and tie a bow. Trim ends into V-notches. Glue assembled tag toward top of ribbon strip on envelope. ∎

SOURCES: Patterned papers and tag stickers from K&Company; Fabri-Tac permanent adhesive from Beacon.

MATERIALS

White and beige card stock
Clear vellum
Assorted holiday
    patterned papers
Embossed tag stickers
White envelope to fit a
    4¼ x 5½-inch card
Mint green envelope to fit
    a 5 x 8-inch card
⅜-inch-wide gold wire-
    edge ribbon
2 (⅛-inch) gold eyelets
    with eyelet setting tool
4 gold round mini brads
Gold ink pad
¹⁄₁₆- and ⅛-inch circle
    punches
Pinking shears
Craft sponge
Permanent fabric adhesive
Glue stick
Computer font (optional)

MATERIALS

4½ x 6-inch red card
Red toile print and green
    striped papers
Red toile print vellum
Vintage Santa and
    Christmas sentiment
    images
Scrap piece of thin
    cardboard
"joy" metal word
¾-inch gold pin back
4 mini round brass brads
Red fiber
⅜-inch-wide burgundy
    organdy ribbon
⅜-inch-wide burgundy
    rib-textured ribbon
Bottle cap
Satin-finish decoupage
    medium
Matte-finish varnish
Brown acrylic paint
Gel stain medium
High-gloss polymer
    compound
1/16- and ⅛-inch circle
    punches
Shape-cutting tool
Tag and 1-inch
    circle templates
Paintbrushes
Paper towels
Acid-free permanent glue
Double-sided
    mounting tape
Clear dimensional
    silicone glue

Christmas Greetings

Design by BARBARA GREVE

Cut a 4 x 5½-inch rectangle from green striped paper and a 4-inch square from red toile paper; with acid-free glue, adhere toile square to striped square, lining up bottom edges. Wrap a piece of burgundy rib-textured ribbon around papers where papers meet, securing ends on reverse side with acid-free glue. Center and glue assembled piece to card.

Use tag template and shape-cutting tool to cut a tag from thin cardboard. Cut a 1-inch-diameter circle around vintage Santa face image; use decoupage medium to attach image inside bottle cap. Allow to dry and apply a coat of matte-finish varnish.

Mix equal amounts of brown paint and gel stain medium. Stain Santa face image with mixture. Wipe stain off with paper towels until desired affect is achieved. Let dry. Following manufacturer's instructions, pour high-gloss polymer compound on top of image. Pour to desired thickness, but do not exceed ⅛ inch. Allow to dry overnight.

Adhere pin back to reverse side of bottle cap with silicone glue. Punch a ⅛-inch hole at top of cardboard tag. Position bottle cap pin below punched hole, allowing room for Christmas sentiment. Mark the two sides of pin back on tag; punch ⅛-inch holes at marks. Attach pin to tag through holes. Adhere Christmas sentiment image below pin. Loop fiber and organdy ribbon through hole at top of tag; trim ends.

Cut a 4½ x 2⅞-inch piece of red toile vellum; lay vellum on bottom front of card. Punch ¹⁄₁₆-inch holes in each corner through vellum; attach brads. Referring to photo for placement, use mounting tape to attach tag to card. Use silicone glue to adhere "joy" metal word in center of red toile vellum. ∎

SOURCES: Patterned papers and vellum from Flair Designs; metal word, ribbons and brads from Making Memories; shape-cutting tool and templates from Fiskars; gel stain medium, decoupage medium, varnish and acid-free glue from Delta; high-gloss polymer compound from Environmental Technology Inc.

Ornament Trio

Designs by KATHLEEN PANEITZ

Cut a 6 x 9-inch piece of white card stock; score and fold in half. Cover front of card with red textured card stock; trim edges even.

Cut a piece of decorative holly border paper slightly smaller than card front. Transfer "Rejoice" in lower right corner. Attach ornaments on left side; attach ornament hangers by inserting a gold brad at the top of each one.

Thread gold ribbon through "happy holidays" tag; tie a knot and trim ends. Attach tag in upper right corner of patterned paper with a gold brad. Transfer decorative circle rub-ons to each gold brad. Glue assembled piece to card.

Use envelope template to trace and cut an envelope from decorative holly border paper; score and fold lines. Glue side and bottom flaps together. Cut a holly border strip from paper; glue along bottom edge of envelope. ∎

SOURCES: Patterned paper and circle rub-on transfers from Creative Imaginations; rub-on transfer and tag from Making Memories; Christmas ornament quilled stickers from EK Success; envelope template from The C-Thru Ruler Co.

MATERIALS

Red textured and white card stock

Decorative holly border patterned paper

Envelope template to fit a 6 x 4½-inch card

3 self-adhesive quilled Christmas ornament embellishments

"happy holidays" tag

"Rejoice" rub-on transfer

Gold brads

Decorative circle rub-on transfers

¼-inch-wide metallic gold ribbon

Glue stick

MATERIALS

Card stock: blue, white,
    metallic gold and dark
    blue rib-textured
Clear vellum
Gold and ivory flecked
    paper
Blue envelope to fit a
    5½ x 4¼-inch card
Rubber stamps: Wise
    men Christmas
    postage stamp, round
    postage symbol, camel
    border and Christmas
    sentiment
Ink pads: purple, gold,
    white and watermark
Yellow colored pencil
Glue stick

Christmas Post

Design by CHRIS NIEMEIER

Cut a 5½ x 8½-inch piece of dark blue card stock; score and fold in half. Use watermark ink to stamp camel border along bottom edge on front of card.

Use purple ink to stamp Christmas postage stamp onto white card stock; trim a rectangle around image and color star yellow. Cut a 2¾ x 1¾-inch rectangle from gold paper; referring to photo, glue to the reverse top portion of image.

Cut a 2⅞ x 1¼-inch rectangle from metallic gold card stock; referring to photo, glue rectangle on the reverse bottom side of image. Layer assembled piece onto blue card stock; cut a 3⅛ x 2¼-inch rectangle around piece. Layer again onto white card stock, trimming a small border. Glue onto vellum; trim a small border and tear off top edge. Glue piece onto card above camel border.

For inside card, cut a 5¼ x 8¼-inch piece of ivory flecked paper; score and fold in half. Glue paper inside card; stamp Christmas sentiment inside with purple ink.

To embellish envelope, stamp camel border at bottom edge with white ink; stamp round postage symbol in gold ink along left edge, overlapping camel border. ■

SOURCE: Rubber stamps from Inkadinkado.

Winter Wonderland

Design by KAREN ROBINSON

Project note: *When using a photo-transfer pen, follow manufacturer's instructions and use in a well-ventilated area.*

Cut a 10½ x 5¼-inch piece of navy blue card stock; score and fold in half. Using photo-editing software, change digital image on computer to black and white; create a feathered border around image. Print image onto white textured card stock. **Option:** *Mat a black-and-white photo of a snow-covered tree onto white textured card stock.* Make a photocopy of image on a toner-based copier, reducing image 25 percent; set photocopy aside. Trim card stock to approximately 2⅞ x 4¼ inches.

Use a computer font or hand-print "Winter Wonderland" onto white textured card stock; trim a rectangle around words, allowing room at each end for a brad. Referring to photo for placement, adhere image and word rectangles to card. Punch a ⅟₁₆-inch hole at each end of word rectangle; insert brads. Machine-stitch around edges of rectangles.

Paint a rough border of silver metallic around edges of card. Wrap fiber through card and around to front positioning fiber between rectangles; tie a knot to secure. Attach snowflake charm above knot with jump ring.

To embellish envelope, place a piece of scrap paper inside to prevent transfer pen from bleeding through. Place photocopied image face down on lower left corner of envelope. Using even pressure, rub transfer pen on reverse side of photocopy until image is transferred, being careful to not move paper until transfer is complete. ∎

MATERIALS

White textured and navy
    blue card stock
Scrap paper
Silver snowflake charm
Silver jump ring
Silver metallic fiber
2 silver mini brads
Silver metallic acrylic paint
Digital winter tree image
    (optional)
Computer with printer
    (optional)
Photo-editing software
    (optional)
Photo-transfer pen
White envelope to fit a
    5¼-inch square card
⅟₁₆-inch hole punch
Sewing machine with silver
    all-purpose thread
Paintbrush
Photocopier
Glue stick

Noel

Design by K A R E N   R O B I N S O N

MATERIALS

Card stock: green, red

Printed paper: red with black text

Transparency sheets

Scrap paper

Rubber stamp: manuscript text

Ink pads: watermark, black solvent-based, metallic gold

Letter templates

Gold ultrathick embossing powder

8 gold decorative clips

1/16-inch-wide metallic gold ribbon

Envelope template to fit a 5¾ x 6-inch card

4 gold round eyelets with eyelet-setting tool

Sewing machine with metallic gold all-purpose thread

Circle punches: 1/16-inch, 5/8-inch, 3/4-inch

Paper adhesive

Cut a 6 x 12-inch piece of green card stock; score and fold horizontal lines 3¼ inches below top edge and 3 inches above bottom edge, forming a bifold card, allowing bottom panel to overlap top panel. Machine-stitch around edges on bottom panel; machine-stitch around side and top edges on top panel.

Using letter templates, trace and cut out letters to spell "NOEL" from scrap paper. Carefully rub watermark ink on top of letters; sprinkle letters with gold ultrathick embossing powder and emboss. Emboss letters again in same manner. Let dry.

Cut four 2⅛ x 2¼-inch rectangles from red card stock. Glue one embossed letter to each square.

Stamp manuscript text onto transparency sheet; let dry. Cut four 2⅛ x 2¼-inch rectangles from stamped transparency. Place a stamped transparency on top of a letter rectangle and using a zigzag stitch, machine-sew transparency to rectangle, sewing along side and bottom edges, leaving top open to form a pocket. Attach a decorative clip to the top of each pocket; secure with glue. Repeat for each letter rectangle.

Referring to photo for placement, glue rectangles to card. Punch two ¾-inch circles from red card stock; ink edges gold. Punch two ⅝-inch circles from red text print paper; ink edges black. Layer small circles on top of larger circles and place one set between the "E" and "L" rectangles toward top of panel; punch a 1/16-inch hole through center of circles. Set eyelet. Repeat with remaining circles, attaching them to top panel between "N" and "O" rectangles. Wrap gold ribbon around closures to close.

For envelope, use template to trace and cut an envelope from red card stock. ***Note:*** *Template measurements may need adjusted slightly to fit card.* Score and fold to form envelope flaps. Punch two ¾-inch circles from green card stock; ink edges gold. Punch two ⅝-inch circles from text print paper; ink edges black. Layer circles together in same manner as for card and attach one set to center of top envelope flap with an eyelet. Layer and attach remaining circle set directly below top envelope flap. Glue side and bottom flaps together. Wrap gold ribbon around circles to close. Cut backs off of four clips; glue fronts to each side of envelope front. ■

SOURCES: Printed paper from 7 gypsies; rubber stamps from Hero Arts; ink pads from Tsukienko Inc.; embossing powder from Suze Weinberg Design Studio; envelope template from Deluxe Designs.

Silent Night

Design by LINDA BEESON

Project note: To apply bleach to stamp, pour a small amount onto a pad of folded paper towels placed in a disposable aluminum pie tin. Tap stamp on paper towels until stamp is covered with bleach. Dispose of towels and pie plate when stamping is complete.

Cut an 8½ x 5½-inch piece of tan card stock; score and fold in half. Cut a 4 x 5¼-inch piece of black card stock; center and glue to card front. Punch out several snowflakes from tan card stock; glue randomly to card, leaving one to be used later.

Using a small amount of bleach, stamp snowman image onto black card stock; let dry. Immediately clean rubber to prevent damage to stamp.

Cut a rectangle around snowman image and glue to tan card stock. Trim a narrow border. Use adhesive foam squares to adhere layered image to right side of card.

Cut a 2-inch length of ribbon; cut ends at an angle. Place ribbon centered behind button; glue ribbon and button to upper right corner of image. Glue remaining tan snowflake beside button.

For envelope, punch a snowflake from black card stock; punch a 1¾-inch circle around punched out snowflake. Glue circle to lower left corner of envelope front. Stamp "warm wishes" several times beside circle using black dye ink. ∎

SOURCES: Rubber stamps from Stampendous and American Art Stamp; snowflake punches from Emagination Crafts.

MATERIALS

Card stock: black, tan
Envelope to fit a 4¼ x 5½-inch card
Rubber stamps: snowman with "silent night," "warm wishes"
Black dye ink pad
Bleach
Cream button
⅜-inch-wide brown/black gingham ribbon
Punches: assorted snowflakes, 1¾-inch circle
Paper towels
Aluminum pie tin
Paper adhesive
Adhesive foam squares

MATERIALS

8 x 3-inch white trifold
    card with 3 precut
    windows

8 x 3-inch sheet of acetate

Envelope to fit an 8 x
    3-inch card

Rub-on transfers: snowmen,
    snow globe, snowflakes,
    candy canes

Iridescent glitter flakes

Silver micro bead/glitter
    mixture

White pearl bead mix

Lime green adhesive beads

Plastic palette knife

¼-inch-wide double-stick
    red tape

½-inch-wide double-stick
    foam tape

Silly Snowmen

Design by VICKI BLIZZARD

With card folded, transfer two snowmen and a snow globe in the centers of the three windows. Transfer snowflake in one window; transfer candy canes to front of window panel as desired.

Cut red tape pieces to fit long card edges; adhere to back of window panel. Do not remove red backing strips at this time. Cut a short piece of red tape to fit between each window and at both ends next to windows. Remove all red backing strips; place acetate sheet over tape. Press firmly to seal.

On back of window panel and on top of acetate, apply ½-inch-wide foam tape, placing long strips of tape along long edges of card. Cut four short strips of foam tape to fit snugly between long strips; place one strip between each window and one strip at each end of card. Do not remove backing strips at this time.

In each window, place a small amount of iridescent glitter flakes, white pearl bead mix and silver micro bead/glitter mixture. Remove backing strips from foam tape and press snowmen panel of card in place over foam tape. Press firmly from front and back sides to form shaker windows.

Use palette knife to apply lime green adhesive beads around each window on front of card; let dry.

If desired, transfer several motifs to front of envelope and envelope flap.

SOURCES: Card and snowmen rub-on transfers from Royal & Langnickel; glitter flakes from Magic Scraps; red tape, bead/glitter mixture and white pearl bead mix from Provo Craft; Liquid Beadz from DecoArt.

Time Flies

Design by STACEY STAMITOLES

Score and fold a 8⅜ x 7½-inch piece of black card stock in half forming a 8⅜ x 3¾-inch card. Cut a 7 x 3-inch piece of ivory card stock; tear bottom edge and apply blue chalk and ink to edges. Center and adhere to front of card.

Use a computer to generate, or hand-print "Time flies when you're having fun!" onto transparency. Follow manufacturer's instructions on shaker box template to form a shaker box from sage green card stock; use printed transparency as the front of the box. Fill shaker box with watch parts and close box with a piece of ivory card stock cut to fit the back opening of box. Mount a strip of magnetic tape onto the back of the shaker box and onto the center of ivory card stock on card. Attach box to card.

For envelope, trace envelope flap onto clock-print paper. Cut out and adhere to flap. Trim a ¾-inch-wide strip of clock-print paper long enough to wrap around bottom of envelope. Wrap strip around envelope and adhere. ∎

SOURCES: Shaker box template from AccuCut; printed paper from Colors by Design; watch parts from 7gypsies; envelope from Making Memories.

MATERIALS

Card stock: black, sage green and ivory
Envelope to fit a 8⅜ x 3¾-inch card
Transparency sheet
Blue ink pad
Blue chalk
Magnetic tape
Clock-print paper
Shaker box template
Assorted watch parts
Adhesive foam tape
Glue stick
Computer font (optional)

Five-Minute Asian Collage Cards

Designs by JUDI KAUFFMAN

MATERIALS

White greeting cards with
    envelopes
Blue mesh
Patterned origami paper
Faux gold Asian coins
Purple and blue ink pads
Large background pattern
    and small motif rubber
    stamps
Piece of mylar or paper
    with punched holes
Double-sided tape
Removable tape
Sponge
Crafting gloves
Cellophane display
    envelopes
Newspaper
Paper glue

The key to making a dozen cards or more in an hour is to assemble supplies before you start and work on all of the cards at once rather than one at a time. Decorating the envelopes adds less than two minutes per card but can add up to $1 to the selling price.

Project notes: All of the cards are one of a kind, even though the same elements were used throughout. The patterned origami paper strips either cross the white "chopstick" lines or echo one of them (for three cards the paper strip hugs the side of a white line). The coins are carefully placed to add balance to each collage. Sometimes what is seen inside the center of the coin is mesh, sometimes origami paper, sometimes half and half—this is not random. Placing the coins is the most time-consuming part of each card, about twenty seconds of consideration.

Speed strategies: I rarely make only a dozen cards at a time. Once I have out my supplies I like to make a large batch! To alter the cards and keep things interesting, change ink colors midway, or choose different rubber stamps. I wear crafting gloves while I sponge or stamp, and while cleaning my sponge and stamps, but remove them for adding collage elements to the cards. Not a second is wasted on washing my hands. Double-stick tape requires no drying time–it's neat and fast.

Altering the project: Instead of Asian papers and coins, choose supplies with a different theme and color palette. To maintain the design, use open mesh, keep the paper strips long and narrow, and the embellishment small and round. The stamps are neutral and abstract. They only appear Asian because of the embellishments.

Cover work surface with newspaper and spread out a dozen blank cards. Attach two strips of removable tape randomly to each card; extend tape past card edges to hold cards in place. Put on gloves and randomly sponge purple ink onto each card; let dry. *Note: Do not clean the sponge.* Place piece of mylar or paper with punched holes onto each card and sponge blue ink through punched holes. Let dry and remove tape. Stamp background pattern onto each card using blue ink; set aside to dry.

Cut desired-size pieces of blue mesh for each card; cut long strips of patterned origami paper. Use double-sided tape to attach origami paper strips and mesh to card in desired arrangements. *Note: Only attach double-sided tape to the center area of mesh where faux coin will hide it.* Attach a coin to each strip.

To decorate envelopes, use blue and purple inks to lightly sponge the punched-hole pattern and small motifs onto each envelope. Cut narrow strips of origami paper the length of the envelopes; attach strips to envelopes. Insert cards and envelopes into cellophane envelopes. ∎

SOURCES: Ink pads from Ranger Industries Inc.; rubber stamps from Red Castle Inc.; crafting gloves from ProCraft; removable tape from 3M.

MATERIALS

Card stock: pearlescent
 light purple, white and
 metallic silver
White mulberry paper
White envelope to fit a
 5 x 7-inch card
Rubber stamps: poinsettia,
 framed poinsettia and
 "Season's Greetings"
Silver microbeads
Clear glitter glue
Pearlescent purple
 embossing powder
Pearlescent purple ink pad
Embossing heat tool
Clear dimensional adhesive
Glue stick

Beaded Poinsettia

Design by CHRIS NIEMEIER

Score and fold a 10 x 7-inch piece of pearlescent light purple card stock in half, forming a 5 x 7-inch card. Stamp framed poinsettia image onto white card stock; emboss with pearlescent purple embossing powder. Cut image out, leaving a small border.

Use clear dimensional adhesive to attach silver microbeads to the center of the poinsettia. Add accent dots to image with clear glitter glue.

Layer stamped image onto silver card stock; trim a ¼-inch border and layer again onto mulberry paper. Tear a small border around image and adhere to card front. Stamp "Season's Greetings" below poinsettia.

For envelope, stamp poinsettia onto lower left corner of envelope. Add accent marks with clear glitter glue. Let dry. ∎

SOURCES: Rubber stamps from Magenta and Duncan; dimensional adhesive from JudiKins.

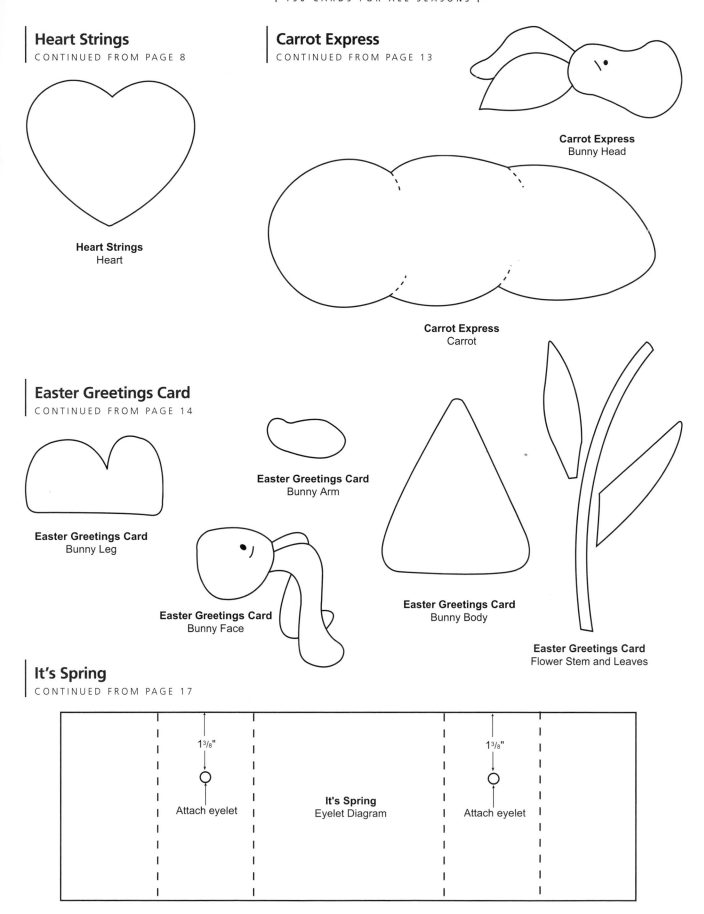

Heart Strings
CONTINUED FROM PAGE 8

Heart Strings
Heart

Carrot Express
CONTINUED FROM PAGE 13

Carrot Express
Bunny Head

Carrot Express
Carrot

Easter Greetings Card
CONTINUED FROM PAGE 14

Easter Greetings Card
Bunny Leg

Easter Greetings Card
Bunny Arm

Easter Greetings Card
Bunny Face

Easter Greetings Card
Bunny Body

Easter Greetings Card
Flower Stem and Leaves

It's Spring
CONTINUED FROM PAGE 17

1³/₈"   1³/₈"

Attach eyelet   Attach eyelet

It's Spring
Eyelet Diagram

Monogrammed Note Cards
CONTINUED FROM PAGE 55

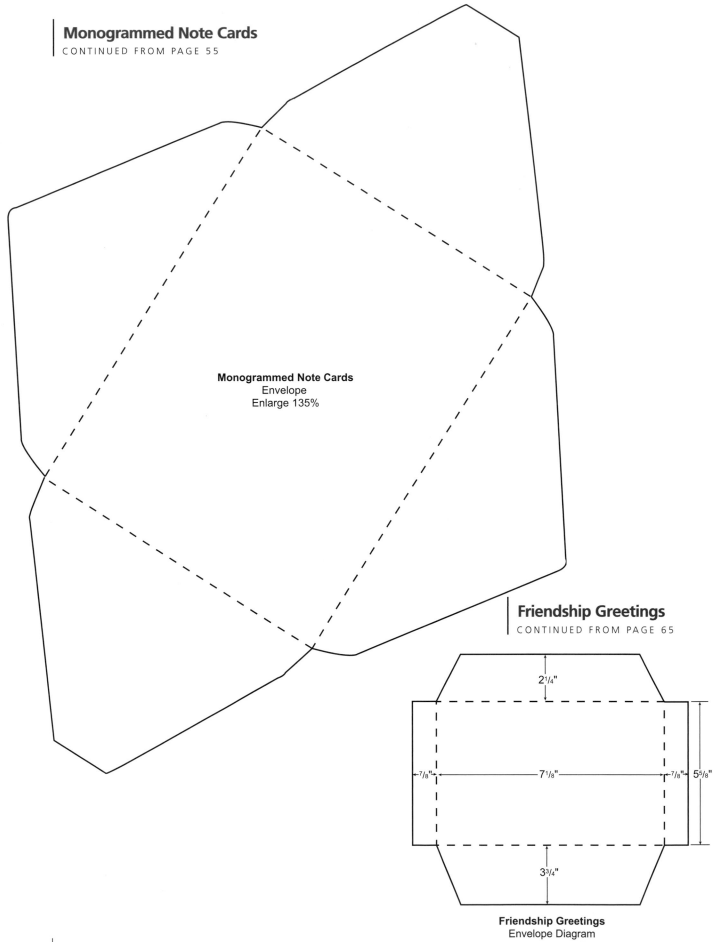

Monogrammed Note Cards
Envelope
Enlarge 135%

Friendship Greetings
CONTINUED FROM PAGE 65

2¼"

7/8" ← 7⅛" → 7/8" 5⅝"

3¾"

Friendship Greetings
Envelope Diagram

Triangle Explosion
CONTINUED FROM PAGE 20

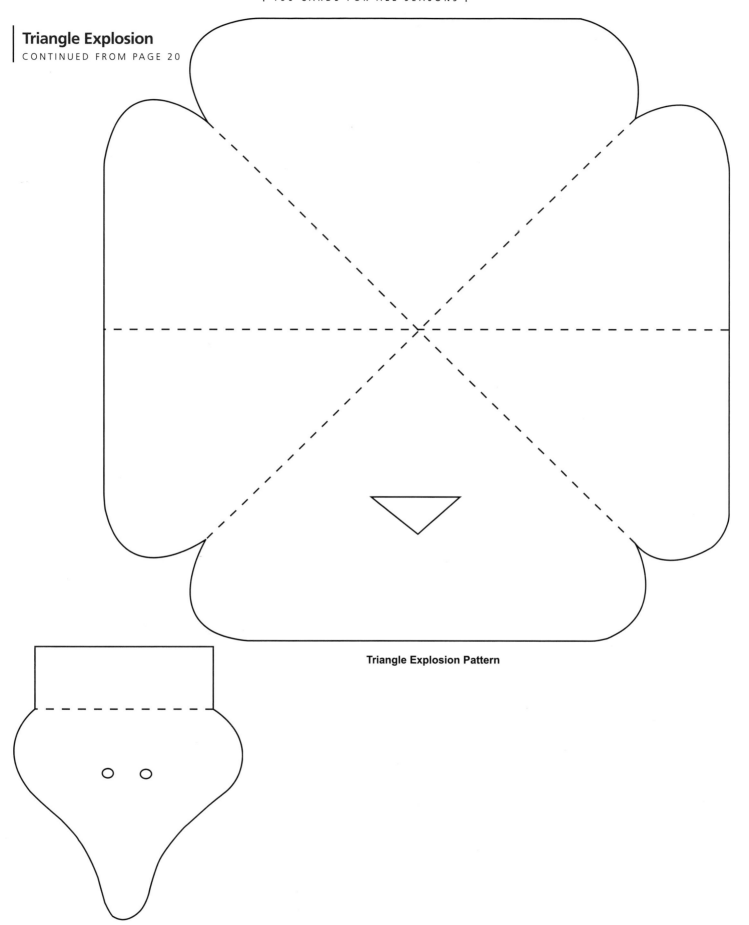

Triangle Explosion Pattern

Triangle Explosion
Closure Flap

Happy Day
CONTINUED FROM PAGE 69

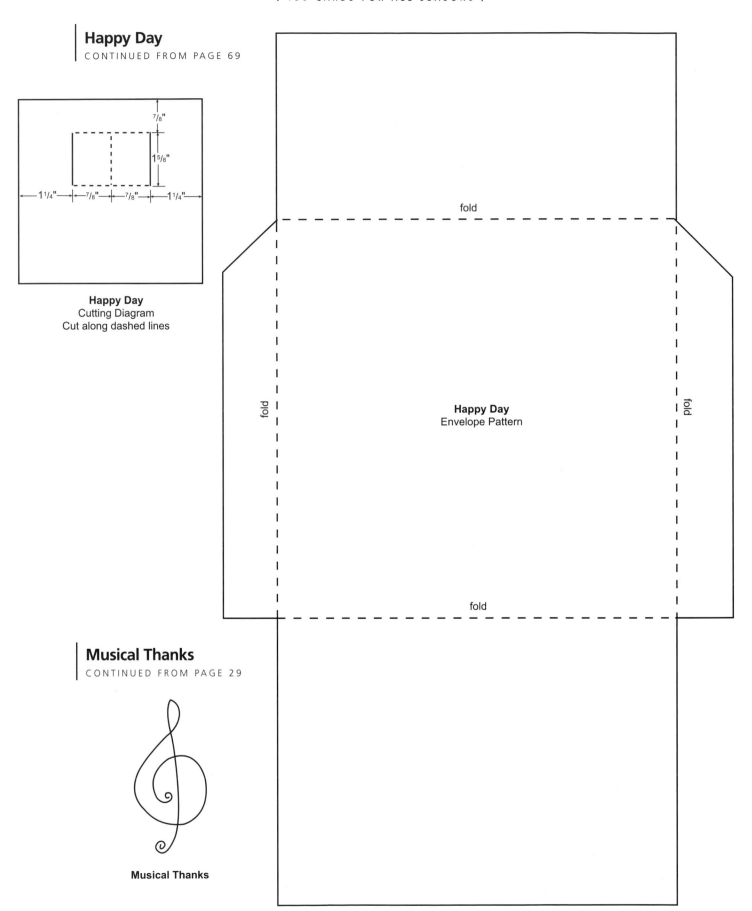

7/8"

1 5/8"

1 1/4"   7/8"   7/8"   1 1/4"

Happy Day
Cutting Diagram
Cut along dashed lines

fold

fold

fold

Happy Day
Envelope Pattern

fold

Musical Thanks
CONTINUED FROM PAGE 29

Musical Thanks

Touch of Elegance
CONTINUED FROM PAGE 108

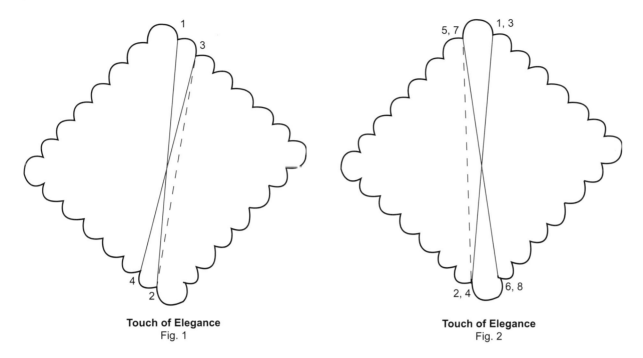

Touch of Elegance
Fig. 1

Touch of Elegance
Fig. 2

Fall Colors
CONTINUED FROM PAGE 110

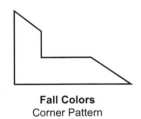

Fall Colors
Corner Pattern

Autumn Delight
CONTINUED FROM PAGE 115

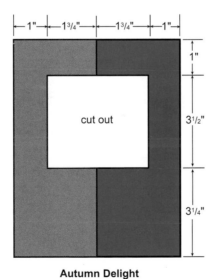

Autumn Delight
Fig. 1

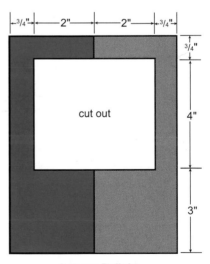

Autumn Delight
Fig. 2

Bunch of Bats
CONTINUED FROM PAGE 123

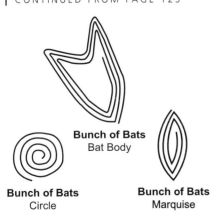

Bunch of Bats
Bat Body

Bunch of Bats
Circle

Bunch of Bats
Marquise

Trick or Treat Trio
CONTINUED FROM PAGE 121

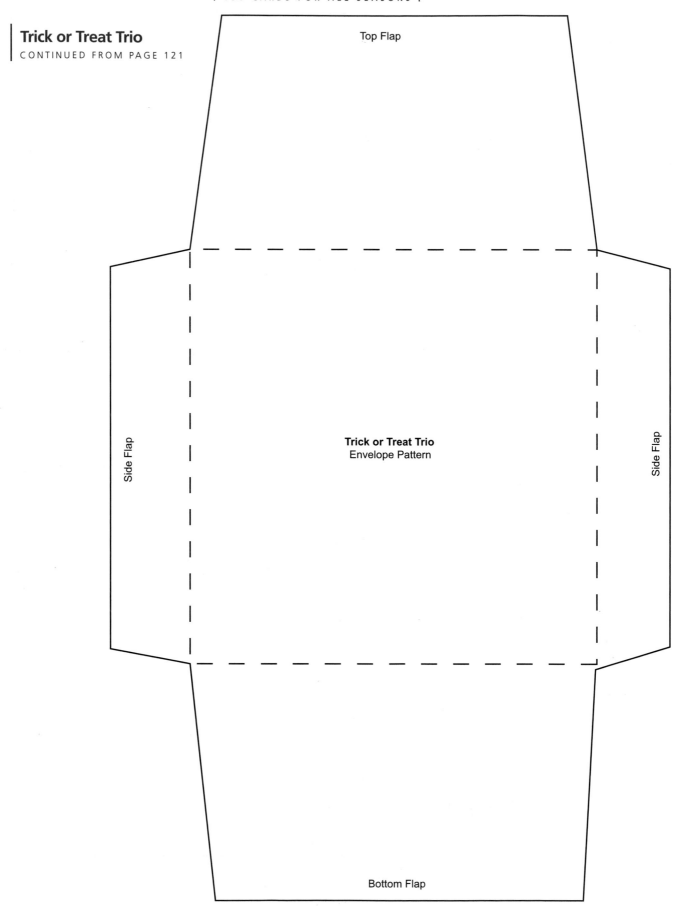

Top Flap

Side Flap

Trick or Treat Trio
Envelope Pattern

Side Flap

Bottom Flap

Holiday Assortment
CONTINUED FROM PAGE 130

Recipes for Christmas
CONTINUED FROM PAGE 137

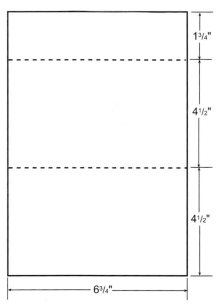

Holiday Assortment
Fig. 1

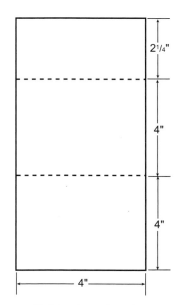

Holiday Assortment
Fig. 2

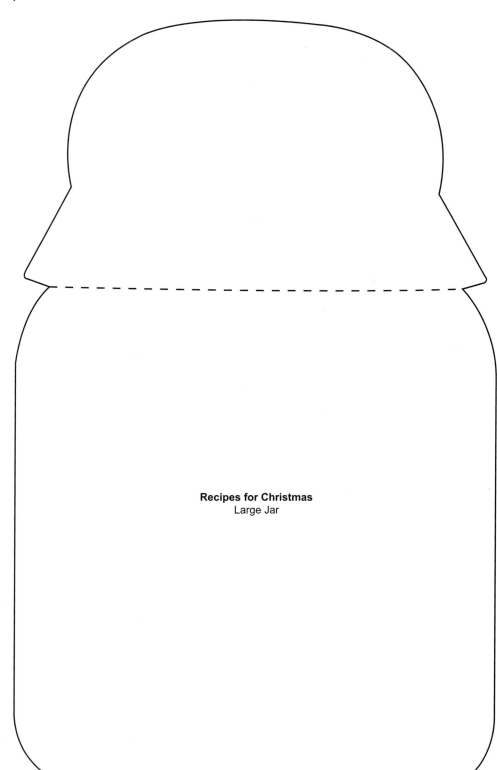

Recipes for Christmas
Large Jar

Recipes for Christmas
CONTINUED FROM PAGE 137

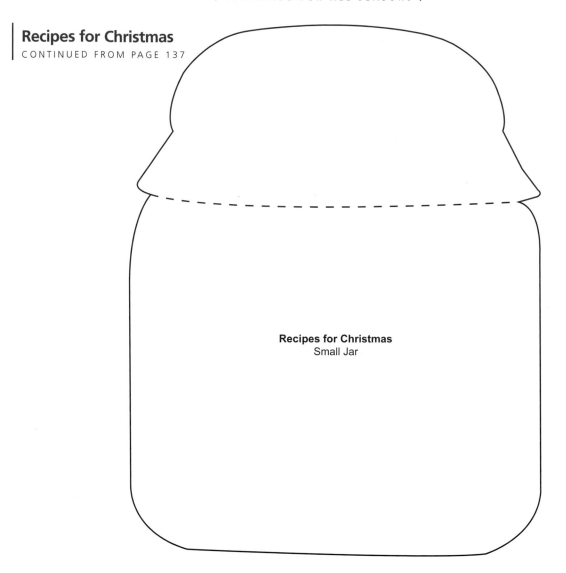

Recipes for Christmas
Small Jar

Buyer's Guide

3M, (866)364-3577, www.mmm.com
7gypsies, (800) 588-6707,
www.7gypsies.com
100 Proof Press Inc., (740) 594-2315,
www.100proofpress.com
A Muse Artstamps, (206) 783-4882,
www.amuseartstamps.com
AccuCut, Customer Care Center,
(800) 288-1670, www.accucut.com
All My Memories, (888) 553-1998,
www.allmymemories.com
American Art Stamp, (310) 371-6593,
www.americanartstamp.com
American Crafts, (801) 226-0747,
www.americancrafts.com
American Tag, www.americantag.com
Anna Griffin Inc., (404) 817-8170,
www.annagriffin.com
Arctic Frog, (479) 636-FROG,
www.arcticfrog.com
Anna Griffin Inc., (404) 817-8170,

www.annagriffin.com
Artistic Wire Ltd., (630) 530-7567,
www.artisticwire.com
Autumn Leaves, (800) 588-6707,
www.autumnleaves.com
BasicGrey, (801) 451-6006,
www.basicgrey.com
Beacon Adhesives Inc., (914) 699-3400,
www.beaconcreates.com
The Beadery, (401) 539-2598,
www.thebeadery.com
Bo-Bunny Press, (801) 771-4010,
www.bobunny.com
The C-Thru Ruler Co./Deja Views,
(800) 243-8419, www.cthruruler.com
Carolee's Creations & Company,
(453) 563-1100, www.caroleescreations.com
Chatterbox Inc., (888) 416-6260,
www.chatterboxinc.com
Clearsnap Inc., (888) 448-4862,
www.clearsnap.com

Close To My Heart, (888) 655-6552,
www.closetomyheart.com
Cloud 9 Design, (763) 493-0990,
www.cloud9design.biz
Colorbök, www.colorbok.com
Colors by Design, (800) 832-8436,
www.colorsbydesign.com
Coronado Island Designs & Stamps,
(619) 477-8900, www.cistamping.com
Craf-T Products, (507) 235-3996,
www.craf-tproducts.com
Creative Imaginations, (800) 942-6487,
www.cigift.com
Creative Impressions, (719) 596-4860,
www.creativeimpressions.com
Creative Paperclay Co, (800) 899-5952,
www.creativepaperclay.com
Daisy D's Paper Co., (888) 601-8955,
www.daisydspaper.com
Darcie's Country Folk, (541) 471-1254,
www.darcie.com

Darice Inc., (800) 321-1494, www.darice.com
DecoArt, (800) 367-3047, www.decoart.com
Decorator's Solution, (800) 261-4772, www.decoratorssolution.com
Delta/Rubber Stampede, (800) 423-4135, www.deltacrafts.com
Deluxe Designs, (480) 497-9005, www.deluxecuts.com
DeNami Design, (253) 437-1626, www.denamidesign.com
Design Originals, (800) 877-7820, www.d-originals.com
Die Cuts With A View, (801) 224-6766, www.diecutswithaview.com
DMD Inc, (800) 805-9890, www.dmdind.com
Doodlebug Design Inc., (801) 966-9952, www.doodlebugdesigninc.com
Dreamweaver Stencils, www.dreamweaverstencils.com
Duncan Enterprises, www.duncancrafts.com
EK Success Ltd., (800) 524-1349, www.eksuccess.com
Emagination Crafts, (866) 238-9770, www.emaginationcrafts.com
Endless Creations Inc., (920) 983-0033, www.shopec.com
Environmental Techology Inc., (707) 443-9323, www.eti.usa.com
Fibers By The Yard, (405) 364-8066, www.fibersbytheyard.com
Fiskars, (800) 950-0203, www.fiskars.com
Flair Designs, (888) 546-9990, www.flairdesiginc.com
Foster/Jarden Home Brands, (765) 281-5000, www.jardenhomebrands.com
FontWerks, (604) 942-3105, www.fontwerks.com
Frances Meyer Inc., (800) 372-6237, www.francesmeyer.com
Fred B. Mullett, (206) 624-5723, www.fredbmullett.com
Green Sneakers Inc., (908) 604-6258, www.greensneakers.com
Hampton Art Stamps, (800) 229-1019, www.hamptonart.com
Heart & Home Inc./Melissa Frances, (905) 686-9031, www.melissafrances.com
Heidi Grace Designs, (866) 89-HEIDI, www.heidigrace.com
Hero Arts Rubber Stamps, (800) 822-4376, www.heroarts.com
Hot Off The Press Inc., (800) 300-3406, www.craftpizzazz.com
Inkadinkadoo, (800) 523-8452, www.inkadinkado.com
Ivy Cottage Creations, (888) 303-1375, www.ivycottagecreations.com
Jesse James & Co. Inc., (610) 865-9530, www.dressitup.com
JewelCraft, (201) 223-0804, www.jewelcraft.biz
JudiKins, (310) 515-1115, www.judikins.com
Junkitz, (7320 792-1108, www.junkitz.com
K&Company, (888) 244-2083,

www.kandcompany.com
Karen Foster Design, (801) 451-9779, www.scrapbookpaper.com
KI Memories, (972) 243-5595, www.kimemories.com
Kreinik, (800) 537-2166, www.kreinik.com
Krylon/Sherwin-Williams Co., (800) 4KRYLO, www.krylon.com
Lasting Impressions for Paper Inc., (800) 9-EMBOSS, www.lastingimpressions.com
Laughing Moon Rubber Stamps, www.laughingmoonstamps.com
LazerLetterz, www.lazerletterz.com
Li'l Davis Designs, (949) 838-0344, www.lildavisdesigns.com
Ma Vinci's Reliquary, www.crafts.dm.net/mall/reliquary
Magenta Rubber Stamps, (800) 565-5254, www.magentarubberstamps.com
Magic Mesh,mail-order source:
My Pajamas On.com, www.mypajamason.com
Magic Scraps, (972) 238-1838, www.magicscraps.com
Making Memories, (801) 294-0430, www.makingmemories.com
Makin's Clay, www.makinsclay.com
Mara Mi Inc., (800) 627-2648, www.mara-mi.com
Marcel Schurman Creations, (707) 428-0200, www.schurmanfinepapers.com
McGill Inc., mail-order source:
Alpine Imports, (800) 654-6114, www.alpineimport.com
me & my BIG ideas, www.meandmybigideas.com
MoBe' Stamps, (801) 439-9806, www.mobestamps.com
Mostly Animals, (800) 832-8886, www.mostlyanimals.com
Mrs. Grossman's, Consumer Relations Department, (800) 429-4549, www.mrsgrossmans.com
My Mind's Eye Inc., (801) 292-0320, www.frame-ups.com
O'Scrap, (801) 225-6015, www.oscrap.com
Paper Adventures, mail-order source:
dMarie Direct, (414) 645-5760, www.dmariedirect.com
Papers by Catherine, (713) 723-3334, www.papersbycatherine.com
Paper Inspirations Inc., (406) 756-9677, www.stampgallery.com
Paper Zone, (877) 92-PAPER, www.paperzone.com
Pebbles Inc., (801) 235-1520, www.pebblesinc.com
Penny Black Inc., www.pennyblackinc.com
Plaid/All Night Media, (800) 842-4197, www.plaidonline.com
Polyform Products Co., (847) 427-0020, www.sculpey.com
Pressed Petals, (800) 748-4656, www.pressedpetals.com
Printworks Collection Inc., (800) 854-6558, www.printworkscollection.com
ProCraft, (888) 776-2738,

www.procraftgloves.com
Provo Craft, mail-order source:
Creative Express, (800) 937-7686, www.provocraft.com
Queen & Co., www.queenandco.com
QuicKutz Inc., (888) 702-1146, www.quickutz.com
Ranger Industries Inc., (732) 389-3535, www.rangerink.com
Red Castle Inc., (877) Red-Castle, www.RedCastle.com
River City Rubber Works, (877) 735-2276, www.rivercityrubberworks.com
Royal & Langnickel, (800) 247-2211, www.royalbrush.com
Rubbernecker Stamp Co., (909) 673-0747, www.rubbernecker.com
Rusty Pickle, (801) 746-1045, www.rustypickle.com
Sandylion, (800) 387-4215, www.sandylion.com
Savvy Stamps, (866) 447-2889, www.savvystamps.com
Scenic Route Paper Co., (801) 225-5754, www.scenicroutepaper.com
Scrapbook Wizard, (435) 752-7555, www.scrapbookwizard.com
Scrappy Cat, www.scrappycatonline.com
Scrapworks Inc., (801) 363-1010, www.scrapworks.com
SEI, (800) 333-3279, www.shopsei.com
Self-Addressed, (866) 300-7474, www.self-addressed.com
Serendipity Stamps, (816) 532-0740, www.serendipitystamps.com
Sizzix/Ellison, (877) 355-4766, www.sizzix.com
The Stamp Doctor, (866) 782-6737, www.stampdoctor.com
Stampabilities, (800) 888-0321, www.stampabilities.com
Stampendous, (800) 869-0474, www.stampendous.com
Stampin' Up!, (800) STAMPUP, www.stampinup.com
Stampington & Co., (949) 380-7318, www.stampington.com
Suze Weinberg Design Studio, (732) 761-2400, www.schmoosewithsuze.com
Technique Tuesday, www.techniquetuesday.com
Two Peas in a Bucket, www.twopeasinabucket.com
Tsukineko Inc., (800) 769-6633, www.tsukineko.com
Uchida of America, (800) 541-5877, www.uchida.com
What's New International/Scrap-Ease, (480) 830-4581, www.scrap-ease.com
Westrim Crafts, (818) 998-8550, www.westrimcrafts.com
Wordsworth, (719) 282-3495, www.wordsworthstamps.com
Xyron, (800) 793-3523, www.xyron.com

The Buyer's Guide listings are provided as a service to our readers and should not be considered an endorsement from *CardMaker* magazine.

Paper Crafting Basics

Paper crafting is easy, creative and fun. Collect basic tools and supplies, learn a few simple terms and techniques, and you're ready to start. The possibilities abound!

Cutting and Tearing

Craft knife, cutting mat Must-have tools. Mat protects work surface, keeps blades from getting dull.

Measure and mark Diagrams show solid lines for cutting, dotted lines for folding.

Other cutters Guillotine and rotary-blade paper cutters, oval and circle cutters, cutters that cut unusual shapes via a gear or cam system, swivel-blade knives that cut along the channels of plastic templates, and die cutting machines (large or small in size and price). Markers that draw as they cut.

Punches Available in hundreds of shapes and sizes ranging from $1/16$ inch to over 3 inches (use for eyelets, lettering, dimensional punch art, and embellishments). Also punches for two-ring, three-ring, coil, comb and disk binding.

Scissors Long and short blades that cut straight or a pattern. Scissors with nonstick coating are ideal for cutting adhesive sheets and tape, bonsai scissors best for cutting rubber or heavy board. Consider comfort—large holes for fingers, soft grips.

Tearing Tear paper for collage, special effects, layering on cards, scrapbook pages and more. Wet a small paintbrush; tear along the wet line for a deckle edge.

Embellishments

If you are not already a pack rat, it is time to start! Embellish projects with stickers, eyelets, brads, nail heads, wire, beads, iron-on ribbon and braid, memorabilia and printed ephemera.

Embossing

Dry embossing Use a light source, stencil, card stock and stylus tool. Add color, or leave raised areas plain.

Heat embossing Use embossing powder, ink, card stock and a heat tool to create raised designs and textures. Powders come in a wide range of colors. Fine grain is called "detail" and heavier called "ultrathick." Embossing powders will not stick to most dye inks—use pigment inks or special clear embossing inks for best results.

Glues and Adhesives

Basics Each glue or adhesive is formulated for a particular use and specified surfaces. Read the label and carefully follow directions, especially those that involve personal safety and health.

Foam tape adds dimension.

Glue dots, adhesive sheets and Cartridge type machines quick grab, no drying time needed.

Glue pens Fine line control.

Glue sticks Wide coverage.

Repositionable products Useful for stencils and temporary holding.

Measuring

Rulers A metal straightedge for cutting with a craft knife (a must-have tool). Match the length of the ruler to the project (shorter rulers are easier to use when working on smaller projects).

Quilter's grid ruler Use to measure squares and rectangles.

Pens and Markers

Choose inks (permanent, water-color, metallic, etc.), **colors** (sold by sets or individually), **and nibs** (fine point, calligraphy, etc.) to suit the project. For journals and scrapbooks, make sure inks are permanent and fade-resistant.

Store pens and markers flat unless the manufacturer says otherwise.

Scoring and Folding

Folding Mountain folds—up, valley folds—down. Most patterns will have different types of dotted lines to denote mountain or valley folds.

Tools Scoring tool and bone folder. Fingernails will scar the surface of the paper.

Paper and Card Stock

Card stock Heavier and stiffer than paper. A sturdy surface for cards, boxes, ornaments.

Paper Lighter weight surfaces used for drawing, stamping, collage.

Storage and organization Store paper flat and away from moisture.

Arrange by color, size or type. Keep your scraps for collage projects.

Types Handmade, milled, marbled, mulberry, origami, embossed, glossy, matte, botanical inclusions, vellum, parchment, preprinted, tissue and more.

Stamping

Direct-to-paper (DTP) Use ink pad, sponge or stylus tool to apply ink instead of a rubber stamp.

Inks Available in pads and re-inker bottles. Types include dye and pigment, permanent, waterproof and fade resistant or archival, chalk finish, fast drying, slow drying, rainbow and more. Read the labels to determine what is best for a project or surface.

Make stamps Carve rubber, erasers, carving blocks, vegetables. Heat Magic Stamp foam blocks to press against textures. Stamp found objects such as leaves and flowers, keys and coins, etc.

Stamps Sold mounted on wood, acrylic or foam, or unmounted (rubber part only), made from vulcanized rubber, acrylic or foam.

Store Flat and away from light and heat.

Techniques Tap the ink onto the stamp (using the pad as the applicator) or tap the stamp onto the ink pad. Stamp with even hand pressure (no rocking) for best results. For very large stamps, apply ink with a brayer. Color the surface of a stamp with watercolor markers (several colors), huff with breath to keep the colors moist, then stamp; or lightly spray with water mist before stamping for a very different effect.

Unmounted stamps Mount temporarily on acrylic blocks with Scotch Poster Tape on one surface (nothing on the rubber stamp) or one of the other methods (hook and loop, paint on adhesives, cling plastic).

Designer Listing & Project Index